What
SUCCESSFUL
Literacy Teachers Do

Outside of a dog, a man's best friend is a book. Inside of a dog, it's too dark to read.

—Groucho Marx

What
SUCCESSFUL
Literacy Teachers Do

(70) Research-Based Strategies for Teachers, Reading Coaches, and Instructional Planners

Neal A. Glasgow ● Thomas S. C. Farrell

CORWIN PRESS
A SAGE Publications Company
Thousand Oaks, CA 91320

For information:

Corwin Press
A Sage Publications Company
2455 Teller Road
Thousand Oaks, California 91320
www.corwinpress.com

Sage Publications India Pvt. Ltd.
B 1/I 1 Mohan Cooperative
  Industrial Area
Mathura Road, New Delhi 110 044
India

Sage Publications Ltd.
1 Oliver's Yard
55 City Road
London, EC1Y 1SP
United Kingdom

Sage Publications Asia-Pacific Pte. Ltd.
33 Pekin Street #02-01
Far East Square
Singapore 048763

Printed in the United States of America

Library of Congress Cataloging-in-Publication Data

Glasgow, Neal A.
What successful literacy teachers do: 70 research-based strategies for teachers, reading coaches, and instructional planners/Neal A. Glasgow, Thomas S. C. Farrell.
    p. cm.
Includes index.
ISBN 978-1-4129-1614-1 (cloth)
ISBN 978-1-4129-1615-8 (pbk.)
1. Reading. 2. English language—Composition and exercises—Study and teaching.
3. Effective teaching. I. Farrell, Thomas S. C. (Thomas Sylvester Charles). II. Title.

LB1050.G56 2007
428.4071—dc22

2006102700

This book is printed on acid-free paper.

07   08   09   10   11   10   9   8   7   6   5   4   3   2   1

Acquisitions Editor:	Faye Zucker
Editorial Assistant:	Gem Rabanera
Production Editor:	Veronica Stapleton
Copy Editor:	Dorothy Hoffman
Typesetter:	C&M Digitals (P) Ltd.
Proofreader:	Carole Quandt
Indexer:	Michael Ferreira
Cover Designer:	Michael Dubowe
Graphic Designer:	Scott Van Atta

Contents

Foreword

In his book, *Ten Trends: Educating Children for a Profoundly Different Future*, Gary Marx foretells the challenges ahead for our society and for educators in particular. In our future, for the first time, the old will outnumber the young. Our nation will be populated by a majority of minorities. Technology will increase the speed of communication and the advancement or decline of our society. Scientific discoveries will force difficult ethical choices, and competition will increase as industries and professions intensify their efforts to attract the most qualified and talented people.

To help the children we now teach to be productive and competitive in the future, educators need to shift their practices and concentrate on those strategies that have the most impact. As the advancements of technology enable humans to progress at a greater rate, time has shortened for educators. There is more to teach children, and far more to learn. One of the trends Marx identified is a growing demand for lifelong learning and continuous improvement in order to function in the ultra-competitive society that is forming all around us.

In this book, Neal Glasgow and Thomas Farrell demonstrate their understanding of the challenges of the future. Knowing that time is crucial, they have created a volume that will allow you, our teachers, reading coaches, curriculum designers, and administrators to zero in on the most productive strategies. The concise organizational structure of the book allows you to quickly increase your knowledge of literacy development, while also creating an opportunity for closer study of specific research that will be most effective with your unique set of children.

Most important, the topic of this book is crucial. Literacy is the most important thing we can give our children. Without the ability to decode, comprehend, write, synthesize information, and think critically, one's chance of succeeding in school and beyond is greatly diminished. In this "future shock" society, a person who lacks this skill set will be lost in the bombardment of information she or he will encounter day by day, minute-by-minute. Imagine trying to navigate the daily challenges in the future, unable to thoroughly comprehend the information on the Internet. How will our children be able to secure jobs and homes for themselves and their children, if their ability to construct and create meaning from text isn't fully developed? How will our nation's government be able to serve the needs of its people, if we can't improve the literacy of the populace? Indeed, as a nation in 2005, only 31 percent of our fourth-grade students scored proficient in reading as tested in the National Assessment of Educational Progress (NAEP) test.

The good news is, the extensive body of research presented in this book demonstrates that all students can learn to read, and teachers have a profound impact on the degree to which the children learn and achieve mastery of educational standards.

Neal and Thomas begin their book with a history of literacy instruction, from the traditional "look-and-say" methods, through the "reading wars" of the 1980s, to the "balanced" approach of the new century. In step with the future trends identified by Gary Marx, the authors next present the reader with strategies to teach literacy in a fashion that makes lifelong learning accessible to the overburdened educator. As the reader pages through the research-based strategies presented, it becomes apparent that the authors are educators who value your time, your capacity to choose the methods that will work for your students, and your need to know more and continue on your professional journey toward continuous improvement of instructional practice.

As a curriculum director of a medium-sized suburban school district, I can see the challenges that teachers are faced with. I reside in a world of "No Child Left Behind" legislation, and I know that although NCLB expectations are challenging, the intention of the law is to benefit *all* children in our charge. Fortunately, the authors of this book understand the challenges that educators face, and they, too, care about *all* the children. They have given us a tool to help with the changes that are ahead of us. I thank them for this volume, and I know you will too.

—Paula Jameson
Curriculum Director
La Mesa-Spring Valley School District

Preface

Teaching reading IS rocket science.

—Louisa Moats

How does one choose what to put in a research-based book on the wide range of literacy topics and concepts in education? Considerable debate exists within the profession regarding specific literacy strategies, but the really good news is that there is a huge body of research to draw from. Educators involved in literacy education—which we hope includes everyone—can pull both inspiration and direction from many academic research perspectives and sources.

Of course, there will always be more to learn about the mechanics of reading, writing, thinking, and other literacy processes. Still, we can now draw from a rich bank of more than 60 years of research to find solutions, resources, and new directions to guide us as teachers in our own class-rooms and as mentor teachers and teacher educators who train and support practicing teachers in their ongoing professional development and in their classrooms. There is no controversy about this.

Educators at all levels need to be well prepared to help a diverse student demographic improve their reading skills. It is the International Reading Association's position (www.IRA.org) that excellent teachers "make a difference in children's reading achievement and motivation to read. That's why every child deserves to have an excellent teacher in her or his classroom." The IRA goes on to characterize successful teachers as those who:

- Understand how literacy develops in children
- Can assess progress and relate instruction to previous experience
- Know a variety of ways to teach reading
- Provide a range of materials and texts for children to read
- Tailor instruction to individual students

Successful teachers also motivate and encourage students as independent learners, have high expectations for achievement, and help learners who are having difficulty.

As educators and authors, we support these goals. Our methodology in writing this book was to seek good research that fosters effective instructional strategies. We hope debate about methodology can be left to other arenas, that those who must take sides in methodology debates continue to value some of what their opposition promotes, and that good teachers continue to choose a variety of instructional approaches to create a balance that works for them and their students.

Successful teachers also know that one of the most important aspects of teaching is to become good at diagnosing the needs of students as individuals. Whether in an affluent suburb, a rural community, or the heart of the urban inner city, successful teachers focus on individual learners and what they bring to the classroom. With the individual learner in mind, debates about one "right way" to teach literacy make little sense. If students already can segment phonemes, why teach that skill again? But if the students cannot hear sounds in words, then it's urgent that we help them acquire the skill. If we keep our focus on learners and their learning needs, rather than just on teaching, we might all have an easier time deciding on literacy methodology and strategy.

The real challenge, as we see it, is to provide many more opportunities for good teachers to access literacy research and effective teaching strategies. That is the purpose of this book. We searched the academic literature to find the best research and the most useful strategies based on sound evidence and our combined experience as classroom teachers and teacher educators. We put our own work through rigorous peer reviews. Our goal has been to use an objective approach that provides teachers with the widest possible range of instructional opportunities to bring to their student-centered learning environments. We believe that no single method or combination of methods can successfully teach all children to read. Because we have not found one clearly documented best way to literacy instruction, we believe educators who are familiar with a broad range of methodologies—and who are closest to their students—must be the ones to make decisions about which instructional methods to use and how to modify them when necessary. That is the major premise of this book. We write for the teachers!

Acknowledgments

I would like to thank our editor, Faye Zucker, for her clear thinking, collaboration, and never-ending support. I would also like to thank my wife, Dr. Peg Just, for her patience, ideas, and support. Finally, I thank the International Reading Association for providing education with a rudder and a well-informed voice!

—Neal A. Glasgow

I would like to thank my wife, Mija, and my daughters Sarah and Ann, who continue to inspire me with their intellect.

—Thomas S. C. Farrell

Corwin Press thanks the following reviewers for their contributions to this book:

Sarah McNary, Faculty, University of Phoenix

Kathleen Prisbell, Teacher of English / Curriculum Council Chair, Russell O. Brackman Middle School, Barnegat, NJ

Patricia Ruggiano Schmidt, Professor of Literacy, Le Moyne College, Syracuse, NY

About the Authors

Neal A. Glasgow has been involved in education on many levels for many years. His experience includes serving as a secondary school science and art teacher both in California and New York, as a university biotechnology teaching laboratory director and laboratory technician, and as an educational consultant and frequent speaker on many educational topics. He is the author or coauthor of eight books on educational topics: *What Successful Teachers Do in Diverse Classrooms: 71 Research-Based Strategies for New and Veteran Teachers* (2006); *What Successful Teachers Do in Inclusive Classrooms: 60 Research-Based Strategies That Help Special Learners* (2005); *What Successful Mentors Do: 81 Researched-Based Strategies for New Teacher Induction, Training, and Support* (2004); *What Successful Teachers Do: 91 Research-Based Strategies for New and Veteran Teachers* (2003); *Tips for Science Teachers: Research-Based Strategies to Help Students Learn* (2001); *New Curriculum for New Times: A Guide to Student-Centered, Problem-Based Learning* (1997); *Doing Science: Innovative Curriculum Beyond the Textbook for the Life Sciences* (1997); and *Taking the Classroom to the Community: A Guidebook* (1996).

Thomas S. C. Farrell is Associate Professor of Applied Language Studies at Brock University in Canada. He has taught at universities in Singapore, Korea, and Canada. His professional interests include reflective teaching, language teacher education and development, and methodology. His recent books include *Succeeding With English Language Learners: A Guide for Beginning Teachers* (2006); *Professional Development for Language Teachers* (with Jack Richards, 2005); and *Reflective Practice in Action: 80 Reflection Breaks for Busy Teachers* (2004).

Introduction

There are many little ways to enlarge your child's world.
Love of books is the best of all.

—Jacqueline Kennedy

Recent staff meeting discourse had just resulted in the introduction of the latest schoolwide effort to foster racial and cultural awareness, the DEAR program: Drop Everything and Read. Once a month, during one class period, a carefully selected article was copied and distributed to every living body on campus, and for 25 minutes everyone had to find a classroom to read, together, an article dealing with racial or cultural awareness. How the reading is done is a matter for the students and the teacher to decide.

This specific day, a group of 9th- and 10th-grade students selected a "popcorn" reading style. Readers completed a paragraph, reading out loud, each one naming a successor for the next paragraph. A couple of patterns quickly emerged. First, the girls in the class tended to be better readers than the boys, and second, many students in the class lacked the confidence to read in front of their peers. Fluency levels varied dramatically. A few students couldn't pronounce or decode common multisyllable words whereas others could read but were simply unable to deconstruct the text to get at the passage's meaning. Before the article was finished, many chronic reading problems were clearly exhibited for all to see. What was now painfully and clearly obvious: even in this high-achieving, high-test-score high school in an affluent suburban setting, reading is still a problem for many students.

This experience was a shock to observers who had expected greater literacy expertise. On reflection, it became clear that teachers probably had been teaching around these students' reading problems for years. With a few exceptions (some students laboriously used phonics to sound out words), most of the struggling readers had little trouble decoding the words. Most of the difficulty was caused by the fact that they had limited vocabularies or lacked the requisite broad background knowledge to apply their reading, and thus they couldn't create meaning. Such students are not always recognized as struggling readers by content teachers, yet they fill our middle school and high school classrooms.

It's clear from the range of reading problems in this single DEAR example that no one system, program, or philosophy can be applied to this specific classroom to meet the needs of all its struggling readers. Instead, the best approach is to offer educators a variety of research-based suggestions, current relevant research summaries, and tested instructional strategies they can choose from for their own classrooms, reading programs, schools, and communities. This approach stresses choosing practices over programs, and current research offers many proven strategies and applications for the specific demographics of your classroom. The format of this book grew out of the need to provide many solutions to the diverse and individual problems teachers face in classrooms worldwide.

This book is not meant to be read as one would read a novel. Rather, our objective is to focus on useful and practical educational research that translates into a range of choices and solutions to individual teaching and learning problems teachers typically face. Within these chapters we present a large range of tips, suggestions, and practices based on studies from research in education, psychology, and sociology. These strategies, suggestions, and practices are designed to help teachers mediate the world of literacy/literacy instruction and make literacy learning easier and more effective for their students. Strategies within the chapters are structured in a user-friendly format:

- The Strategy: A simple and concise statement of a teaching tip.
- What the Research Says: A brief discussion of a journal article or book from peer-reviewed research literature that led to the tip. This section should simply give the teacher some confidence in, and a deeper understanding of, the principle(s) being discussed as the "teaching tip."
- Classroom Application(s): A description of how this teaching tip can be used and applied in instructional settings.
- Precautions and Possible Pitfalls: Caveats intended to make implementation of the teaching tip reasonably error free. We try to help teachers avoid common difficulties before they occur.
- Source(s): One or more sources are provided so that interested readers may refer to the original research.

We hope all teachers will benefit from the practical classroom applications we have filtered through research findings and our own experience as educators. We know that new teachers receive advice and support from colleges and universities, mentors, veteran colleagues, and induction programs. This book's intention is to bring teachers advice and support from the educational research literature as well. It's likely that any teacher—first year or veteran—reading this book for the first time will find strategies that don't apply. As in any new endeavor, teachers new to embedding literacy in their curriculum may tend to "not know what they don't know." We ask that you come back and revisit this book from time to time throughout the year. What may not be applicable the first time you read it may be useful at a later date.

Teaching and education in general have never been more exciting or more challenging. Expectations for teachers, learners, and literacy levels continue to rise. The more strategies teachers can use to assist students along their journal to literacy, the better the outcome for us all. We hope all educators find this book a practical and useful addition to their collection of teaching resources.

1

The Very Complex and Often Controversial History, Philosophy, and Theory of Reading and Literacy

Literacy arouses hopes, not only in society as a whole but also in the individual who is striving for fulfillment, happiness, and personal benefit by learning how to read and write. Literacy . . . means far more than learning how to read and write. . . . The aim is to transmit . . . knowledge and promote social participation.

—UNESCO Institute for Education, Hamburg, Germany: *The Search for Solid Ground*

Research regarding literacy comes in many shapes and sizes, and it is conducted for a wide range of purposes. The most reliable research is most often presented in peer review format. The phrases "research-based" or "evidence instruction" are often used to validate a practice or a program. The validity of any program is reflected in the quality of the research that supports it. The various sources used to summarize the historic trends in literacy often cite peer review research, especially information coming from the *National Reading Panel Report—Teaching Children to Read: An Evidence-Based Assessment of the Scientific Research Literature on Reading and Its Implications for Reading Instruction.* In the United States and around the world, considerable public attention has and continues to be given to literacy instruction, and contentious discussion about how best to meet the literacy-related needs of children and adults often occurs. These exchanges and debates over research results, research conclusions, and instructional practices often reflect strong and contrasting philosophical perspectives. The tracking of research trends and political and educational philosophical perspectives over time can provide a context for anyone developing his or her own philosophy or classroom practices. There is great value in knowing where others have been, and you can benefit from their experiences. The history of literacy education is a good place to start looking for understanding.

This introductory chapter breaks with the overall format of this book but is necessary to give you an idea of how literacy philosophy, theory, research, and instructional practice have evolved over the years. Thus, it helps you create a context when developing your own ideas about literacy and how to teach it by providing you with some points of reference for many of the strategies we present in this book. By becoming more aware of the history of thought on the subject of literacy education, we hope to help set the stage for conversation about current and future thinking on literacy and related topics. The following text, then, presents a short chronological summary of the major evolutionary points of literacy education during last 90 years.

Early Twentieth Century

In the United States in the late twenties, the beginning curricular materials most schools used were usually based on the word or "look-and-say" instructional method, making Dick, Jane, and Spot household names along with the characters in the early Dr. Seuss books. An examination of word-based beginning readers, which were supposedly based on the philosophy of reading for meaning, shows a remarkable lack of intellectual content with trite storylines students would find working with as unattractive and boring as the meaningless repetition of letters. Phonics instruction was sometimes taught, but this depended on the training and interest of one's teachers.

During this period the phrase "functional literacy" began to be used to describe a very basic level of literacy needed to function in all but the most menial jobs. The tests given to American recruits during World War I showed that about 25 percent were unable to read and write well enough to perform simple assigned tasks. The newly formulated standardized tests at the time continued to reveal such results as a distressingly high percentage of eighth-grade students who could read only at a third-grade level. High school teachers regularly criticized primary and elementary teachers for this low level of language skills, and the colleges and universities in turn deplored the reading level of their incoming students. We sometimes hear the same complaints today. Often, a failure to develop language skills was blamed on teaching methods rather than on the overall learning conditions of community demographics, class size, resources available, or home and social environments. To compound these problems, many teachers were not very well educated themselves.

After World War II, criticism of the large proportion of functionally illiterate in the United States, estimated at the time to be one third to one half of adults, grew until it reached its peak with the publication in 1955 of Rudolf Flesch's influential book, *Why Johnny Can't Read*. A common counterargument at the time, and indeed one still heard today, is that the aims of education were far more than teaching the "three R's," yet public concern soared. After World War II, the main educational development efforts were focused on expanding formal schooling. It was assumed that higher rates of school attendance would help end the "scourge" of illiteracy.

Many critics of educational theory saw the ability to read and write as absolutely fundamental to education. Their main complaint and target was the word *method*; to them "look-and-say" was really "look-and-guess" (as opposed to "drill-and-kill," which came along later). According to critics at the time, because children were not being taught word attack skills, they were handicapped in decoding and deciphering new words and therefore could not handle further education. Reading philosophy and theory then moved into another transition period during the fifties and sixties.

The 1950s and 1960s

During the fifties, the instructional strategy of choice was to teach children to just decode print, and most believed understanding and comprehension would follow easily and naturally. Pedagogy centered on phonics, and the phrase "sound it out" was commonly heard in classrooms and homes across America. Flashcards drills and word attack strategies were common. Rote memorization and drill and practice were the strategies of choice, whereas the most common alternative strategy reverted to the "look-say" method.

In the sixties, the number of studies on the teaching of reading soared. Some accounted for the high adult illiteracy rate by simply a lack of practice. Although adults were able to "read," in work and everyday situations they read very little, thus remaining at a very fundamental level of reading: because they didn't use their reading skill, they lost it. Of those studies comparing different teaching methods, the majority supported some sort of phonics approach. However, we caution readers that many of these studies were limited in approach, and the researchers' conclusions may even have been distorted by vested interests such as a relationship with a publishing company. Reading instruction during the sixties was defined as decoding print only; learning sound-symbol relationships and word recognition was considered the best approach to reading. Spelling, handwriting, and written composition often were not integrated into reading instruction and were taught separately.

The 1970s

In the seventies, though decoding and phonics did not completely disappear, there was a new trend toward reading for meaning. Ethnic diversity became a new educational issue, and "ESL" (English as a second language) was added to the literacy agenda. Reading was beginning to be seen as a more complex process than decoding, involving more than just looking at print words on a page. Reading graphs and diagrams, using indexes, and locating information in nonfiction books were added to the literacy paradigm. The trend toward widening the literacy paradigm also included reading in genres beyond fiction as well as developing research and library skills.

Reading was now seen as a metacognitive activity with some integration of spelling, handwriting, and composition. The terms semantic, syntactic, and graphophonic came into the professional literacy discourse for the first time and contributed to a go-for-meaning philosophy. Now literacy teachers asked students to predict the meaning of unknown words rather than just sound them out. Syntactic knowledge gave students a feel for grammar, and students read and reread trying to construct meaning. Comprehension was not seen as the end result, but just part of beginning to construct meaning. Miscues in spelling and pronunciation were now sometimes accepted as long as meaning was established.

The 1980s

In the early eighties, the supposedly miraculous results of Marie Clay's "Reading Recovery" program in New Zealand became an inspiration to those who were uncomfortable with or rejected the repetitious, teacher-directed instruction broken up into small packages of language arts, and the *whole-language* concept began a new era in literacy instruction. Reading Recovery itself draws on both phonics and whole-language theory, but in America it has served as a transmission device for whole language only. Clay's Reading Recovery specifically, and whole language reading instruction generally, spread quickly through literacy instruction circles during the eighties. The founders of the whole-language paradigm—Frank Smith, for many years a professor of psychology at the University of Victoria, in British Columbia, and Kenneth Goodman, a professor of education at the University of Arizona—saw themselves as champions of teachers who were up against a hostile world. They presented whole-language instruction as a joyful, humanistic, and intellectually challenging alternative to deadening phoneme drills, where the classroom was turned from a factory floor into a nurturing environment in which children naturally blossom.

Advocates claimed it was more than an instructional method, it was also a philosophy. Reading should not be taught but acquired through the student actually reading real books, following as the teacher reads, using context, pictures, and known words to understand even if every word is not familiar. Student motivation rather than instruction was key, and instructional methods were to be child centered rather than teacher centered or directed. While phonics would still be taught incidentally, teaching separate language skills (encoding, decoding, and spelling) in isolation was now rejected. Interestingly, the philosophy and methods of the progressive education movement of the early 1900s are rarely mentioned in literature on whole language. Educational jargon changes, yet some programs look surprisingly familiar.

The converts rejected any suggestion that it was just a revival of the look-and-say method. They believed that if meaning and motivation were present, the child would learn to read as naturally as he or she learned how to talk. As class sizes and diversity of student demographics grew, the whole-language approach provided some relief. Some teachers saw the technique as much easier to teach within the changing demographics. Despite opposition from a few who said its success was unproven, its appeal was so seductive that many schools (such as the California system in 1987) and most teacher-training institutions fully embraced it. Soon phonics-themed books were hard to find in schools, and new teachers usually had no background in teaching phonics.

But the paradigm's momentum was not to last, for the emphasis soon swung back away from whole language. In the United States, the "reading wars" and debates over the best teaching methods expanded from the educational arena into the realm of politics and even religion. In their nostalgia and frustration at what they perceived as their children's inadequate development of language skills, many parents became a ready market for sales of phonics books and commercial tutorial schools. Many saw poor spelling in particular as an indication that the "new" methods were unsatisfactory.

Two distinct theoretical and pedagogic camps were established during this period: a phonics and decoding camp and a reading-for-meaning, whole language camp. Although many people support phonics simply because they believe it works better, it has also been a longstanding cause of the political right and in a number of communities it is one of the main organizing issues for the Christian Coalition. Whole language has generally been a cause of the left and the more progressive thinkers. Thus, reading instruction and curriculum became increasingly politicized.

Professionally, teachers leaving school in the seventies and early eighties did not have the same background in the teaching of reading as teachers in the fifties and sixties. In addition to sound-symbol relationships, predicting and confirming strategies, reading and rereading, and the use of visual context were added as strategies. Reading materials began to expand to include other media beyond books, including text sources from outside the classroom.

Literacy skills in general, and reading/writing specifically, were seen as a much more complex task in the eighties. Reading and writing above a functional level was beginning to be seen as necessary in most jobs. Accountability and standardized testing became a greater part of professional discourse because of the Bush (senior) administration's focus on testing. Controversies continued over phonics and decoding and other philosophies of literacy teaching and learning. The teaching, or not teaching, of spelling and the practice of "invented" spelling were also controversial. Student writing was seen by some as too personal, and a call for the "back to basic" movement began to be heard on the national level. The problem with this approach was lack of agreement on what was really basic. Basics skills and job requirements change from generation to generation. What was considered literate in the eighties was different from definitions in the sixties and before. The focus on structure of texts forced teachers to examine syntactic systems, what knowledge about syntax and grammar should be taught, and what students need to know to be considered literate as the concept evolved. The media began to report that standards were falling and students were leaving school unprepared for the literacy requirements of the time. However, within the definition of literacy and unlike earlier times, reading and writing were usually seen on equal terms. Writing was seen as composing meaning into text and reading as composing meaning from text.

The 1990s

In the nineties, the literacy pendulum began to swing once again. The death of whole language began with California's new state reading test, administered in 1993 and 1994, which turned out to be a political disaster. Passages about oppression, taken from the work of Alice Walker among other writers, generated furious opposition from the right, and Governor Pete Wilson canceled the test in 1994. But the scores were released and showed disastrously low levels of reading proficiency: 77 percent of fourth graders read below their grade level. By the time these shocking scores came out, the 1994 elections had given California a Republican-majority state assembly for the first time in years, and the elementary school curriculum became a new political issue. The consensus was that embracing whole language had been a huge mistake. The newly elected state super-intendent of public instruction, Delaine Eastin, quickly distanced herself from whole language and set up a task force on reading and math that recommended more emphasis on phonics and computational skills.

In the fall of 1995 the legislature passed, without a single dissenting vote in either house, two bills mandating the use of instructional materials that teach reading through phonics and math through "basic computational skills." Professional development quickly turned away from anything related to whole language; this trend then quickly moved to other states.

Also in the nineties, the term literacy continued to evolve, assimilating speaking, listening, and critical thinking into the realm of reading and writing. Literacy was taken to be the ability to read and use written knowl-edge and to write appropriately. In addition, the early nineties saw a mas-sive information explosion, and the age of technology began to require a much more complex set of literacy skills than had been necessary in the past. Analysis of multimedia communication now became part of the lit-eracy paradigm, and critical thinking was seen to be a very valuable skill. Literacy instruction in the nineties also began to be viewed as a life-long pursuit (preschool to adult) as people need, adopt, and practice new skills after they leave the formal classroom.

Early Twenty-First Century

Transitioning from the nineties, the current period is considered the age of multiliteracies as meaning-making requires complex skills that could not have been imagined in the fifties and the sixties. The definition of literacy has grown well beyond text reading, writing, and spelling. For example, based on the idea that visual images are a "language," visual literacy can be defined as the ability to understand and produce visual or text and visual messages. This skill is becoming increasingly important with the ever-proliferating mass media and the Internet. As more and more information and entertainment is acquired through nonprint media (such as television, movies, and the Internet), the ability to think critically and visually about the images presented becomes a significant skill. The ability to process visual images efficiently and understand their impact on viewers is very important. There is much we and our students need to learn about new semiotic systems. What literacy practices and skills work best in teaching these multiple semiotic systems? They are being developed as we go. Also during this period of standardized testing accountability, politics and politicians have taken much more control of the literacy agenda, and those without high levels of literacy are seen as more likely to become a "burden" to society. Literacy pedagogy exists more and more outside the school's boundaries and within political discourse.

Meaning-making at the beginning of the twenty-first century now involves the ability to "read" print in addition to multimedia presentations and complex visual representations. Information comes in much more complex packages than ever before. Today, the term that seems to be used most regarding literacy instruction practice is the "balance approach." While not specifically naming it, the International Reading Association describes the approach this way:

> The International Reading Association has developed position statements on several important issues related to beginning reading instruction, including statements about phonics and phonemic awareness as well as a joint position statement with the National Association for the Education of Young Children, called Learning to Read and Write: Developmentally Appropriate Practices for Young Children (1998). The purpose of this position statement is to clarify the Association's stance on methods for teaching beginning reading (hereafter referred to as reading methods). A reading method is a set of teaching and learning materials and/or activities often given a label, such as phonics method, literature based method, or language experience method.

> The essence of their position is as follows:

> There is no single method or single combination of methods that can successfully teach all children to read. Therefore, teachers must have a strong knowledge of multiple methods for teaching reading and a strong knowledge of the children in their care so they can create the appropriate balance of methods needed for the children they teach. (International Reading Association Position Statements, 2006)

The association comments further on who should decide the content of beginning reading instruction:

> Because there is no clearly documented best way to teach beginning reading, professionals who are closest to the children must be the ones to make the decisions about what reading methods to use, and they must have the flexibility to modify those methods when they determine that particular children are not learning.

We still don't really know exactly what the term "balanced approach" means, and any consensus might be hard to reach. A balanced approach could be described as "mixing some phonics with whole language," but how this is accomplished in any particular classroom is unclear. This eclectic approach, as some have come to call it, sometimes involves teaching phonics first, and then "graduating" to a whole-language approach. Alternatively, the phonics instruction may be explicit, but children might be given more opportunities to read connected, authentic literature. Or lessons prescribed by phonics and whole-language pedagogy may be intermixed in the hopes that different children will benefit from different "styles" and methods of teaching.

Reading Proficiency Levels in 2005

Nationally, students in more than 17,600 schools in the United States participated in the Nation's Report Card's (2005) reading assessment, which was administered from January to early April 2005 to more than 165,000 students at Grade 4, to 159,000 students at Grade 8, and to 12,000 students at Grade 12. On a 0 to 500 point scale, fourth graders' average score was 1 point higher and eighth graders' average score was 1 point lower in 2005 than in 2003. Average scores in 2005 were 2 points higher than in the first assessment year, 1992, at both Grades 4 and 8.

Between 1992 and 2005, there was no significant change in the percentage of fourth graders performing at or above *Basic,* but the percentage performing at or above *Proficient* increased during this time. The percentage of eighth graders performing at or above *Basic* was higher in 2005 (73 percent) than in 1992 (69 percent), but there was no significant change in the percentage scoring at or above *Proficient* between these same years.

The average scores for White, Black, Hispanic, and Asian/Pacific Islander students increased between 1992 and 2005. Looking at the short-term trend, Black and Hispanic students each scored higher on average in 2005 than in 2003. The White-Black and White-Hispanic score gaps narrowed during this same time. Students who were eligible for free or reduced-price school lunch and those who were not eligible had higher average scores in 2005 than in 1998. In the short term, students who were eligible showed a 2-point increase from 2003 to 2005. In 2005, female students scored higher on average than male students. Male students' average score increased by 3 points from 1992 to 2005.

At the national level, *No Child Left Behind* reflects literacy concerns with the new program called *Reading First.* An ambitious national initiative designed to help every young child in every state become a successful reader, it is based on the expectation that instructional decisions for all students will be guided by the best available research. Under Reading First, states can receive significant federal funding to improve reading achievement. Funds are made available for state and local early reading programs that are grounded in scientifically based research. In such programs, students are systematically and explicitly taught the following five skills (defined by National Reading Panel, 2000), identified by research as critical to early reading success:

- *Phonemic awareness:* the ability to hear and identify sounds in spoken words.
- *Phonics:* the relationship between the letters of written language and the sounds of spoken language.

- *Fluency:* the capacity to read text accurately and quickly.
- *Vocabulary:* the words students must know to communicate effectively.
- *Comprehension:* the ability to understand and gain meaning from what has been read.

Research has consistently identified the critical skills young students need to learn in order to become good readers (National Reading Panel, 2000). Teachers across states and districts have demonstrated that scientifically based reading instruction can and does work with all children. They have made children—even those among the most difficult to educate—proficient readers by the end of third grade. Thus, the key to helping all children learn is to help teachers in each and every classroom benefit from the relevant research. That can be accomplished by providing professional development for teachers on the use of scientifically based reading programs; by using instructional materials and programs that are also based on sound scientific research; and by ensuring accountability through ongoing assessments. We hope this book can provide insight into much of the recent research into literacy instruction.

Sources

The International Reading Association Position Statements. Accessed July 2006 at: http://www.reading.org/

Learning to Read and Write: Developmentally Appropriate Practices for Young Children (1998). A joint position of the International Reading Association (IRA) and the National Association for the Education of Young Children (NAEYC). Available at: http://www.naeyc.org/

National Center for Educational Statistics (2005). *Reading: The Nation's Report Card.* Available at: http://nces.ed.gov/

National Reading Panel Report: Teaching Children to Read: An Evidence-Based Assessment of the Scientific Research Literature on Reading and Its Implications for Reading Instruction (2000). Available at: http://www.nichd.nih.gov/

Schnorr, R. & Davern, L. (2005). Creating exemplary literacy classrooms through the power of teaming. *The Reading Teacher, 58,* 494–506.

Turbill, J. (2002). The four stages of reading philosophy and pedagogy: A framework for examining theory and practice. *Reading Online, 5*(6). Available at: http://www.readingonline.org/

U.S. Department of Education. (2002). *No Child Left Behind (NCLB).* Available at: http://www.ed.gov/

2

Phonics, Phonemics, and Decoding

You don't have to burn books to destroy a culture. Just get people to stop reading them.

—Ray Bradbury

 Strategy 1: "Sound it out": Coach word recognition in beginning reading.

What the Research Says

Kathleen Clarke (2004) points out that in the early primary grade classrooms, word recognition can present a major challenge for readers. So she suggests that teachers actively coach their students for this word recognition task and that this coaching strategy views young readers as active learners. Clarke (2004, p. 442) proposes that, to be a successful coach with word recognition exercises, they should provide readers with more detailed information about the word-recognition task itself by focusing the readers' attention on graphophonic knowledge, and word-part identification strategies and relevant contextual supports. For example, she suggests that the grapheme phoneme strategy asks the students to consider individual letters and sounds in words such as, "Does the 'or' sound like 'or' in corn or in actor?" Reading teachers next encourage their students to locate the individual phonograms. Clarke (2004) then suggests that the use of contextual supports focuses readers' attention on the inappropriateness of a miscue when they are reading; for example, the teacher can say, "You said taking [thinking] of ways."

Classroom Applications

 According to Clarke, word recognition coaches should make three points when designing cues to support word recognition: First, teachers should realize that word recognition relies heavily on graphophonic knowledge in that words are recognized by attending to the environment in which they are placed. Second, it is important that cues be clear and direct, focusing on reading words, not learning rules. Third, teachers should consider the language they use to coach the students and not make it incomprehensible. In these ways, reading teachers can have a specific strategy based on word recognition by having the students sound out each word and then asking them appropriate questions about those words. After students repeatedly and actively participate, they will begin to recognize the words they are reading.

Precautions and Possible Pitfalls

 Coaching groups of students may be problematic if the teacher does not keep the groups small and flexible, because students do not all progress at the same rate and some may need individual coaching. In addition, students and groups may need to be coached repeatedly and not in a one-off event. Coaching word recognition should take place a few times each week for effective results.

Source

Clarke, K. (2004). What can I say besides "sound it out": Coaching word recognition in beginning reading. *The Reading Teacher, 57,* 440–449.

Strategy 2: Teach phonemic awareness and phonics in the classroom and at home.

What the Research Says

Sharon Darling (2005) suggests that when teachers and parents partner to support children's reading and academic achievement, at-risk children can show a lot of gains not only in terms of personal reading pleasure but also on reading tests. One way of doing this is to have classroom instruction in phonemic and phonic awareness reinforced with home instruction by parents.

Classroom Applications

 Darling (2005) proposes the following two-step process that both teachers and parents can use in implementing this strategy. First, phonemic awareness instruction improves children's word reading, reading comprehension, and spelling. Teachers can employ any number of strategies in the classroom for such instruction, including the use of songs, rhymes, poems, and chants: working with syllables. The next step is to support such instruction at home, and Darling suggests that parents can reinforce it by any of the following means:

- Sing alphabet songs with their child.
- Read stories that their child chooses.
- Help their child clap the beats or syllables in words.
- Point out letters, especially letters in their child's name.
- Play with language and rhymes.
- Sing songs that manipulate phonemes, such as "The Name Game."

For systematic and explicit phonics instruction in the classroom to improve students' word recognition, spelling, and comprehension, Darling proposes that teachers use such strategies as helping children relate letters to sounds and decode words in stories. Then at home, she suggests parents can reinforce phonics classroom instruction by encouraging their children to point to words and say them out loud when writing, helping their children define larger words by breaking them into smaller chunks, and playing spelling and word games such as Scrabble and Hang Man.

Precautions and Possible Pitfalls

It is very important that teachers talk to and instruct parents in how to carry out home reinforcement of these two reading strategies; otherwise both parents and their children may become confused about such instruction, which in turn may have negative consequences for classroom instruction. Teachers may consider holding classes for parents before they embark on these strategies to avoid misunderstanding about what is required to make this work and why.

You may also find some parents are not strong readers themselves. You will need to be very sensitive with these parents and not embarrass them. Go slowly so as not to threaten them and their relationship with their children.

Source

Darling, S. (2005). Strategies for engaging parents in home support of reading acquisition. *The Reading Teacher, 58,* 476–479.

Strategy 3: Use decoding to improve word identification problems and improve fluency.

What the Research Says

According to John Pikulski and David Chard (2005), the notion of fluency in reading needs to encompass more than just oral reading; they suggest that it also encompass the idea of fluency as freedom from word identification problems that tend to cause comprehension problems. If we include this decoding to improve word identification problems, they say, it enlarges our understanding of reading fluency to include comprehension and not just oral reading. However, they point out that the relationship between fluency and comprehension is not as simple as it sounds because of the unresolved issue of whether fluency is an outgrowth of, or a contributor to, comprehension. That said, Pikulski and Chard (2005) suggest that reading fluency is indicated in accurate, rapid, expressive oral reading and is applied during, and makes possible, silent reading comprehension.

Classroom Applications

Pikulski and Chard (2005) suggest reading teachers teach high-frequency vocabulary. Such words appear many times in our language—the, of, and, at, to—and if beginning readers cannot instantly identify these words, they are unlikely to become fluent readers. Posting high-frequency vocabulary on word walls and practicing them, Pikulski and Chard maintain, may help these developing readers.

Precautions and Possible Pitfalls

Pikulski and Chard (2005) caution that high-frequency words in themselves are often seen as problems in that many demand decoding skills because they are phonically irregular. For example, while the word "have" does not follow the generalization about the effect of a final *e* on a preceding vowel sound, the *h, v* and *e* all behave as they should, and the *a* does represent a sound that it often represents. Consequently, teaching high-frequency words can be a difficult undertaking requiring reading teachers to point out the regular elements of irregular words in order to help children recognize them instantly.

Source

Pikulski, J., & Chard, D. (2005). Fluency: Bridge between decoding and reading comprehension. *The Reading Teacher, 58,* 510–519.

 ## Strategy 4: Use drama rhymes to teach reading.

What the Research Says

 Betty Roush (2005) maintains that learning nursery rhymes is an important first step toward literacy for developing readers, as they are a key to phonological development. By dramatizing nursery rhymes through words and actions, students are developing their oral language and phonological awareness. Roush (2005) points out that nursery rhymes have a musical quality with different language patterns, rhythm, and rhyme in the verses, and as such they help children satisfy their fascination with language patterns and encourage their language development. Furthermore, she points out that phonological awareness is a powerful predictor of whether students will be successful in reading.

Classroom Applications

Roush (2005) suggests that when beginning the process of drama rhymes, teachers should select a rhyme familiar to the students. Each line of the nursery rhyme is then examined to determine which words can be dramatized. Realia or pictures can also be used to help students understand words or concepts. Roush (2005) uses the example of the nursery rhyme "Humpty Dumpty" as follows: for the first line, "Humpty Dumpty sat on a wall," a wall on the school grounds can be used to help the children experience where Humpty Dumpty was. "All the king's horses" is a difficult concept because some children may never have seen a horse. Teachers can use videos or pictures that show horses galloping to help the children understand horses. For "All the king's men," teachers can use pictures of soldiers, and talk about their role in relation to the king. For "Couldn't put Humpty together again," teachers can bring in an uncooked egg and drop it into a container to demonstrate what happens to Humpty Dumpty. After completing the dramatization, teacher and students can explore the rhyming words.

Precautions and Possible Pitfalls

 Selecting a rhyme that is familiar and common to second-language learning students may be very difficult for the teachers, maybe even defeating the purpose of using drama rhymes in the first place. Multicultural classrooms present a unique problem in finding rhymes all students can relate to.

Source

Roush, B. (2005). Drama rhymes: an instructional strategy. *The Reading Teacher, 58*, 584–587.

 Strategy 5: Consider visual-syntactic text formatting for digital text as a technique for increased academic achievement and long-term reading proficiency.

What the Research Says

 Walker and coworkers (2005) noted that over 60 million U.S. workers now spend more that two hours a day reading directly from a computer screen. They also explained that more than 70 percent of college and university students prefer to conduct research online and only 9 percent prefer the traditional library. Because of the type of literacy demands today, these researchers were looking for a method to aid people in reading electronic documents that would reduce eyestrain and increase comprehension.

Walker's group explored the use of visual-syntactic text formatting (VSTF) for its potential to help readers identify grammatical structure. VSTF helps readers identify syntactic structure by changing the way electronic writing is displayed. VSTF breaks the text into shorter rows, usually 8 to 30 characters, that fit into one or two eye fixation spans. The eye can capture a width of only about 9 to 15 characters of text at each fixation, and this method helps break complex syntax into more readable phrases. It also varies the indentation patterns that guide the eyes from row to row. This makes it easier to follow sequential text both visually and intellectually.

What makes this all possible is the fact that digital text, unlike print text, can be displayed in a variety of shapes, sizes, and colors with no increase in production costs. The VSTF method uses algorithms that identify the most important phrase boundaries in a sentence to break the sentence into shortened segments. The algorithms also use rules that cluster words and phrases into larger phrase groups based on the syntactic attributes of each word.

Walker's group hypothesized that the VSTF method could enhance retention and comprehension in college and high school readers. They explored the use of VSTF with 48 college students in an introduction to psychology class. A majority of college students preferred the VSTF format to the conventional format, citing reduced eyestrain, and ease of reading and review, which all improved their grades.

They also used VSTF technology with 50 ninth-grade high school students in world history classes. The students read a digital version of the textbook formatted in VSTF. Comparing the pilot VSRF classes' scores on a variety of assignments with those of historical and concurrent control groups with a traditional text showed a full standard deviation increase in scores with VSTF.

Visual-syntactic formatting immediately helped college students read challenging material more effectively and efficiently. It eliminated eyestrain and helped 30 to 40 percent of first-year students who required remedial instruction. For high school students, it improved both immediate and long-term retention of content area textbooks and improved reading proficiency. It helped readers over a broad range of reading aptitudes.

Classroom Applications

This technology is relatively new and not readily available, yet the results of the Walker et al. study make the technology hard to ignore. This study provides evidence that a model of syntactic parsing and sentence decoding is a key underpinning of reading fluency. Increased fluency serves as a connection between word decoding and greater comprehension.

The VSTF method and format create a new paradigm for electronic publishing and new possibilities for educators. The program's overall feasibility has yet to be determined. Cost comparisons between books and computer technology need to be made. The exact proportion of curricular time needs to be examined also. In-class reading time was used in this study. It was estimated that reading time took up to 20 percent of total class time. An analysis of class time versus reading time and textbook cost versus computer-based electronic text cost needs to be made. You can access a parsing service at http://www.liveink.com/. It is worth exploring this technology.

Precautions and Possible Pitfalls

It is hard to predict the future of visual-syntactic text formatting. The research and the paper referenced do present a promising picture of an emerging technology. It is certainly not a mainstream idea at this point but may be worth exploring or keeping an eye on. Remember, most currently used technology started outside the mainstream!

Source

Walker, S., Schloss, P., Fletcher, C. R., Vogel, C. A., & Walker, R. (2005). Visual-syntactic text formatting: A new method to enhance online reading. *Reading Online, 8(6)*. Available at: http://www.readingonline.org/

3

Vocabulary, Spelling, and Word Study

The failure to read good books both enfeebles the vision and strengthens our most fatal tendency—the belief that the here and now is all there is.

—Allan Bloom

Strategy 6: Revisit and reconsider the role that vocabulary instruction plays in comprehension and reading motivation.

What the Research Says

In the large scheme of literacy instruction, Joshi (2005) and Harmon, Hedrick, and Wood (2005) feel that vocabulary development and the role it plays in reading skills acquisition have received much less attention than decoding and comprehension strategies. Joshi goes on to state that there is a close relationship between vocabulary and comprehension; hence individuals with poor vocabulary have difficulty understanding written text. Carrying the idea further, students with poor vocabulary knowledge read less and acquire fewer new words. In contrast, students with better vocabulary read more and improve their comprehension (the Matthew effect), Joshi (2005) states that to prevent the Matthew effect from taking hold, vocabulary assessment and instruction needs to be an important component of reading programs, especially for the struggling readers.

All the source studies contain some review of the literature on vocabulary instruction and its role within other literacy components. They also explore the ebb and flow of vocabulary instruction in classrooms over the years as it has fallen in and out of favor.

Classroom Applications

A common theme running through the cited research states that vocabulary instruction is important but an ignored teaching skill. The researchers go on to argue about the important relationship between vocabulary (the amount of words children are exposed to from very early years) and the many other instructional concepts related to literacy.

Joshi (2005) also talks about the discrepancy between oral and reading vocabulary. In spite of large oral vocabularies (45,000 for an average high school graduate), reading vocabularies are drastically smaller. According to Biemiller (1999), only about 300 words are learned in a year through direct vocabulary instruction. One explanation for this low number is that poor readers tend to read easier material and fewer books, consequently poor readers' vocabularies grow at a slower pace. In contrast, students with bigger vocabularies read more, comprehend better, and thus read still more, increasing their vocabularies.

At present, vocabulary is often taught by asking students to do some form of glossary search or definition search in the dictionary. Dictionary-based or rote-memory vocabulary instruction is noted for short-term retention in contrast to meaning-based approaches, which results in more lasting memory and better overall comprehension.

Examples of meaning-based alternatives beyond dictionary-based approaches are as follows (Joshi, 2005):

Instructors can embed targeted words in sentences and draw the student's attention to the context. Sentences with missing words could be utilized to have students find words from the context of the sentence supplied to them.

If it fits your teaching style, the use of antonyms and synonyms can also make words meaningful.

Again if it fits your style and knowledge background, common morphemic roots can provide students with insights into word meanings. For example, if you know the meaning of "rupt" (to break), you can begin to give students the tools to unlock meaning with words such as abrupt, interrupt, corrupt, and erupt.

Word origin, or etymology, also can offer paths to meaning-based strategies. The fact that words have a history you can share with students provides a context and a "hook" to begin to mentally attach a word to an authentic context. Old English or Anglo-Saxon words are common in elementary reading materials. These are high-frequency words, which comprise 15 percent of the English language and are acquired easily. The Greeks also gave us about 15 percent of English words. These tend to be specialized word found in the sciences. About 60 percent of English words come from Latin and are found everywhere and in every content area. Relating the stories behind the words helps give the words a "presence."

A variety of word or concept mapping or webbing activities can be used to support the active processing of new words. Students can expand their vocabularies, and begin to understand the concepts between words and context ideas. These activities and strategies can be used as part of a prereading activity, a during-reading activity, or a postreading activity. In a prereading context, as a visual display, they serve to activate and begin to construct important concept ideas before the reading begins. These activities between the development of vocabulary and reading comprehension reinforce the connection between the two concepts.

Once you train yourself to teach from these strategies you will offer your students a richer experience and a stronger "glue" for retaining the use of vocabulary words. Because fluent reading is largely determined by a reader's stock of sight words, it is logical to believe that stronger vocabulary knowledge will yield greater fluency in reading.

The common goal in these strategies is drawing the student's attention to word meanings. Words meaningful to students are more easily learned and retained than if they are only memorized. Knowing there is a gap between a student's receptive and expressive vocabulary, keep in mind that using words is more important than just knowing them. Teachers need to encourage their students to use as many of their receptive vocabulary as possible to help solidify the words in their memories.

For more strategies, information, and instructional tips on vocabulary visit the Education Development Center's Literacy Matters website (http://www.literacymatters.org/). It is one of the largest collections of vocabulary-based teaching ideas on the Internet.

Precautions and Possible Pitfalls

Creating arbitrary vocabulary lists that have little to do with other learning in the class is not a good idea. If students are not actively engaged in individual use and discussion of words, you're working against students encountering words in a meaningful way. Teaching words and vocabulary strategies that are functionally important within a specific context, and in the context of actual books, fosters vocabulary development and long-term retention.

Sources

Biemiller, A. (1999). *Language and reading success*. Cambridge, MA: Brookline Books.

Harmon, J. M., Hedrick, W. B., & Wood, K. D. (2005). Research in vocabulary instruction in the content areas: Implications for the struggling reader. *Reading & Writing Quarterly, 21*, 261–280.

Joshi, R. M. (2005). Vocabulary: A critical component of comprehension. *Reading & Writing Quaterly, 21*, 209–212.

Rupley, W. H., & Nichols, W. D. (2005). Vocabulary instruction for the struggling reader. *Reading & Writing Quarterly, 21*, 239–260.

Strategy 7: Use teacher "read-alouds" as an effective practice for enhancing two of the critical components of reading instruction.

What the Research Says

A student's range of vocabulary has been shown to be an important indicator of how fluent a reader the student can be. English-language learners are one of the largest groups of students who struggle with such problems in literacy, especially because of their limited vocabulary understanding. Peggy Hickman, Sharolyn Pollard-Durodola, and Sharon Vaughn (2004) suggest that integrating the teaching of word meanings with the content area makes instruction more beneficial than teaching vocabulary separately as a list of words and definitions. Hickman, Pollard-Durodola, and Vaughn (2004) suggest that classroom teachers use teacher read-alouds as a consistent activity because they provide frequent, it not daily, opportunities to enhance the literacy of English-language learners (ELLs). Specifically, they suggest that vocabulary can have a powerful impact on students' skill development in literacy.

Classroom Applications

Hickman, Pollard-Durodola, and Vaughn (2004) suggest that both narrative and informational trade books can be used for read-alouds, and they should be chosen at a reading level one or two grade levels above the students' grade placement. They should also be chosen on the basis of students' interests and needs. Furthermore, each book can be separated into passages of 200 to 250 words, thus breaking with the natural flow of the story, and particularly important or challenging vocabulary reviewed on the day after the last passage is read and discussed, with the teacher reading the complete book over a week. Each read-aloud session should be about 30 minutes; by dividing texts into smaller units, or passages, the teacher is able to focus on a smaller number of vocabulary words to adequately explore their meaning(s) as they were used in the context of the story. For selection of vocabulary, Hickman, Pollard-Durodola, and Vaughn (2004) suggest teachers focus on words of high utility that can be used across contexts, and words that go beyond familiar or basic vocabulary but are not so abstract and technical that their use is limited. They suggest that lessons can be designed as follows:

- Introducing (previewing) the story and three new vocabulary words
- Reading a passage from a narrative or informational text out loud, focusing on literal and inferential comprehension
- Rereading the passage, drawing attention to the three vocabulary words
- Extending comprehension, focusing on deep processing of vocabulary knowledge
- Summarizing what was read and any content knowledge that was learned

Precautions and Possible Pitfalls

 As with most lessons that focus on vocabulary development, teachers should be cautious about how many words they introduce at any one time and the difficulty of the words chosen, because no two students ever have the same vocabulary ability.

Source

Hickman, P., Pollard-Durodola, S., & Vaughn, S. (2004). Storybook reading: Improving vocabulary and comprehension for English-language learners. *The Reading Teacher, 57,* 8, 720–730.

 ### Strategy 8: Use semantic impressions to teach vocabulary.

What the Research Says

 Margaret Richer (2005) notes that vocabulary knowledge is among the best predictors of reading achievement, but more often that not, vocabulary instruction is tedious and ineffective.

Richer (2005) observed that studies show words must be processed deeply and repeatedly by students and are typically learned gradually, and the more deeply students process words, the better they learn them. She notes that students internalize meanings by using words in a certain order, to compose their own story before they read the printed story, so the teacher should choose key words from a story or book chapter and list them in the order in which they appear. She calls this the use of semantic impressions to teach vocabulary.

Classroom Applications

 To make learning words fun, interactive, and empowering, Richer (2005) suggests using the semantic impressions teaching strategy. Teachers choose between 5 and 20 words that are central to the plot of a narrative (story, book chapter). They list these words, in the order in which they appear in the story, on a chalkboard or overhead, and then ask the students, as a group, to compose a sensible story (with a beginning, middle, and end) using these words. The teachers can quickly go over each word's meaning, and students are told the following:

1. Words must be used in order.

2. Once a word is used, it can be reused.

3. The form of words (plurals, tenses, parts of speech) can be changed.

As students contribute orally, teachers write their semantic impressions story on the chalkboard or overhead. (Note that the word list, as well as the story, is displayed.) When the story is finished, the class may choose to edit it. Have the students read, or listen to, the published narrative.

Precautions and Possible Pitfalls

To keep a cohesive hold on the class, teachers may want to break up the students into small groups, rather than have students tell their stories in one large group; they can then record each group's story and write it on the board or an overhead later for presentation in a future class.

Source

Richer, M. (2005). Words are wonderful: Interactive time efficient strategies to teach meaning vocabulary. *The Reading Teacher, 58*, 414–423.

Strategy 9: Use word expert cards to teach vocabulary.

What the Research Says

Margaret Richer (2005) has pointed out that it is important for teachers to address word learning directly with instruction in word meanings. However, she says that in typical reading classrooms the usual practice is to have students look words up in a dictionary, copy or restate definitions, and then create sentences using the words, though the students often cannot understand these definitions or may not know how to choose the appropriate definition from multiple meanings. She suggests that teachers use the strategy of word expert cards to teach vocabulary, to make it fun and interesting; this strategy allows each student to be a word expert for some of words to be learned during a class. Students construct word cards, thus gaining experience in interpreting dictionary definitions, then they teach one another the words so that later, when they see the words in the context of a novel, meanings are reinforced and deepened. The strategy of word expert cards thus combines direct vocabulary instruction, word study in context, and peer teaching.

Classroom Applications

The teacher starts by identifying a master list of key words (50 to 100) that are in general use, and each student is assigned two or three different words from the list. The students then make word expert cards for their two or three personal words in the following steps described by Richer (2005): First, each student writes the word and copies the sentence containing the word from the book. Next, the student looks up the word in a developmentally appropriate dictionary and finds the part of speech and meaning that matches the way the word is used in the copied sentence. The student now writes the definition, in his or her own words, and finally writes a personal sentence using the word. When the cards have been approved by the teacher, the students use them to teach their words to their classmates while working in pairs. After the pairs have completed their teaching task, students rotate to another partner and repeat the process.

Precautions and Possible Pitfalls

The only two problems that may be associated with this strategy for teaching vocabulary are that the teacher chooses the words to be studied, and not the students (ownership problems), and the peer teaching process takes a lot of time, although it may be time well spent.

Source

Richer, M. (2005). Words are wonderful: Interactive time efficient strategies to teach meaning vocabulary. *The Reading Teacher, 58,* 414–423.

Strategy 10: Whether you develop your own word-study/spelling approach or teach with a published program of some type, you need to match the specific system with the developmental stages of the learners.

What the Research Says

 Templeton and Morris's (2001) examination of spelling development and instruction is part of a larger work, the *Handbook on Reading Research: Volume III* (Kamil, Mosenthal, Pearson, & Barr, 2000). They began with a look at the historical and contemporary context for spelling research and instruction, broken down into a variety of contextual categories for spelling pedagogy from the mid-1800s on. Pedagogy ranged from spelling and reading being closely related in the nineteenth century to separating in the twentieth century. Spelling pedagogy has been seen as a process of rote memorization. The idea is that the English spelling is irregular and that its acquisition is best achieved primarily through rote memorization.

Classroom Applications

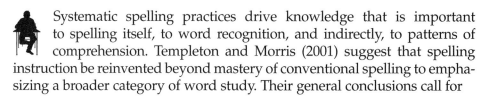 Systematic spelling practices drive knowledge that is important to spelling itself, to word recognition, and indirectly, to patterns of comprehension. Templeton and Morris (2001) suggest that spelling instruction be reinvented beyond mastery of conventional spelling to emphasizing a broader category of word study. Their general conclusions call for

- More reading and writing to advance spelling ability.
- Greater encouragement of invented spelling in the early years. Once students begin to explore spelling on a regular basis, they should be encouraged to look for patterns.

- Inductive or exploratory practices that are appropriate for all students. For the most struggling spellers, a more deductive, systematic, and direct approach is appropriate.
- An emphasis on interrelatedness of spelling and phonics, word morphology, and vocabulary as students develop their ability. This emphasis should include the explicit presentation and a discussion of how the look of a word and its meaning are represented in the spelling system.
- A spelling pedagogy that allows for different progress rates because students develop differently. Instruction should reflect and connect to students' spelling level, not their grade level.
- Teachers who know the spelling system and their students' stages of spelling development.

Precautions and Possible Pitfalls

 The role of spelling and spell checkers in the lives of students is open for debate today. Invented spelling and spell checkers call for new skills that blend technology and a variety of other spelling philosophies. Everyone, including parents, has his or her own ideas regarding the role of spelling within the literacy paradigm. Be mindful of the related politics.

The problem of gender equality in spelling also needs to be addressed. Girls are still found to perform significantly better than boys, at all grade levels. How can spelling philosophy accommodate this disparity? There are no really good answers here.

Sources

Allred, R. A. (1990). Gender differences in spelling achievement in grades 1 through 6. *Journal of Educational Research, 83,* 187–193.

Groff, P. (1994). Recent spelling for research: Some implications for spelling reform. *Journal of Simplified Spelling Society, 1,* 3–7.

Kamil, M. L., Mosenthal, P. B., Pearson, P. D., & Barr, R. (Eds.). (2000). *Handbook on Reading Research: Volume III.* White Plains, NY: Longman.

Sipe, R., Walsh, J., Reed-Nordwall, K., Putman, D., & Rosewarne, T. (2002). Supporting challenged spellers. *Voices from the middle, National Council of Teachers of English, 9*(3), 23–32.

Templeton, S., & Morris, D. (2001). Reconceptualizing spelling development and instruction. *Reading Online, 5*(3). Available at: http://www.readingonline.org/

4

Fluency

Frederick Douglass taught that literacy is the path from slavery to freedom. There are many kinds of slavery and many kinds of freedom. But reading is still the path.

—Carl Sagan

 Strategy 11: With the right strategies, reading fluency can be improved in middle and high school classrooms.

What the Research Says

 Rasinski and coworkers (2005) suggest that problems with reading fluency go well beyond elementary school. They found that lack of reading fluency appeared to be the greatest problem and reading impairment in students referred for supplementary reading instruction by their classroom teacher. This lack of fluency also accompanied comprehension problems in referred students. While their research primarily used reading rate as a measure in assessing reading fluency, they clearly defined fluency as also including reading accurately for meaningful phrasing and expression. They wanted teachers to be wary of programs that seek only to boost reading rate and not comprehension.

Classroom Applications

 Rasinski and coworkers (2005) suggest that it is not difficult to integrate reading fluency into regular classroom instruction. Reading fluency develops with contextual reading practice. Guided reading of instructional materials with emphasis on repeated reading of the same material, a form of reading practice, is one of the most powerful ways to increase fluency and comprehension, and it transfers to other material not previously encountered. This strategy is best accomplished through performance activities, that is, putting students in a position to perform for others. Most students are naturally inclined to practice to a point where they can read passages accurately, with appropriate rate and expression and phrasing. Meaningful expression is especially important when reading poetry, scripts, oratory, and songs, which are meant to be performed. With thought and creative planning, students can be engaged in repeated reading.

Students will learn what a teacher teaches. Fluency has been generally seen as a problem for elementary teachers and students. Students in middle and high schools rarely get fluency support. With a little work, teachers can integrate fluency strategies into many content areas and fluency instruction will improve content retention so that teachers are not trading content instruction for reading instruction. They can compliment one another.

Precautions and Possible Pitfalls

Many students are self-conscious about their reading skills. It is very important for a teacher to consistently provide a safe and nurturing environment. Students will feel more comfortable and take more risks with less anxiety.

Also, beware of programs that focus only on reading rates and the students do not comprehend what they read.

Source

Rasinski, T. V., Padak, N. D., McKeon, L. G., Wilfong, J. A., & Friedaur, P. H. (2005). Is reading fluency a key for high school reading? *Journal of Adolescent & Adult Literacy, 49*(1), 22–27.

Strategy 12: Let learners read as much as possible.

What the Research Says

 Richard Day and Julian Bamford (2004) suggest that the most critical element in learning to read is the amount of time spent actually reading. The problem is how to get our students reading as much as possible if they cannot choose the materials they want to read. As Day and Bamford (2004) suggest, we need to be able to cultivate a reading habit in our students so that they will move from learning to read to reading to learn.

Classroom Applications

 Day and Bamford (2004) point out that there is no upper limit to the amount of reading that can be done, but a book a week is probably the minimum amount of reading necessary to achieve the benefits of extensive reading. As all our learners will be at different proficiency levels, we must find ways of keeping their interest. Any of the following activities may be useful:

- Have the learners write a description of any of the characters.
- Ask them why they chose that particular character and what helped with composing the description.
- When they have finished, all the different descriptions can be posted on a bulletin board for the whole class to read.

Teachers can also have the class write a letter to a classmate about a book they are reading and why they should also read it. The class can even be encouraged to write a letter to the author of the book they are reading and give their views on the book. This makes the whole process of writing book reviews real and hopefully they will get a reply from the author.

Precautions and Possible Pitfalls

 Each of our learners will be invariably at different proficiency levels and so it may be difficult to get them to read a book a week if they do not find suitable materials.

Source

Day, R., & Bamford, J. (2004). *Extensive reading.* New York: Cambridge University Press.

Strategy 13: We are all reading teachers and we should act as reading role models.

What the Research Says

 Most researchers on extensive reading agree that successful extensive reading teachers are voluminous readers themselves. In other words, they teach by example by displaying to their students that they also read every day. They are displaying to their students that they belong to a community of readers and they can even read what their students are reading to show them that they too are interested in the students' chosen topics.

Classroom Applications

 A simple, yet most effective way of selling extensive reading is for the teacher to bring in some reading material to class and read each time the students are reading. This way the teacher can model reading behavior (rather than telling them to read) by showing them how he or she reads and what material was chosen. The teacher can also make it a point to be seen reading during lunch time on the school grounds and in other strategic locations.

Precautions and Possible Pitfalls

Apart from taking care with the type of reading materials the teacher brings to school, we see no major pitfalls with this strategy.

Source

Day, R. & Bamford, J. (2004). *Extensive reading.* New York: Cambridge University Press.

Strategy 14: Keep in mind the three key elements of reading fluency: accuracy in word decoding, automaticity in recognizing words, and the use of meaningful oral expression and learn how to address them within instruction.

What the Research Says

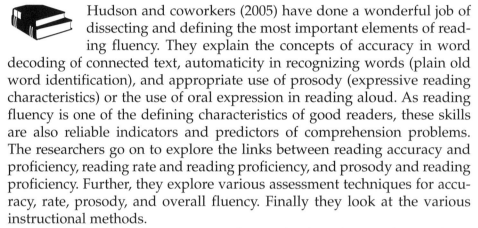 Hudson and coworkers (2005) have done a wonderful job of dissecting and defining the most important elements of reading fluency. They explain the concepts of accuracy in word decoding of connected text, automaticity in recognizing words (plain old word identification), and appropriate use of prosody (expressive reading characteristics) or the use of oral expression in reading aloud. As reading fluency is one of the defining characteristics of good readers, these skills are also reliable indicators and predictors of comprehension problems. The researchers go on to explore the links between reading accuracy and proficiency, reading rate and reading proficiency, and prosody and reading proficiency. Further, they explore various assessment techniques for accuracy, rate, prosody, and overall fluency. Finally they look at the various instructional methods.

Rasinski's 2006 paper critiques the work of Hudson and coworkers, validating much of what they said, but with some concerns regarding instructional priorities implied in their article. Hasbrouck and Tindal (2006) simply examined the use of oral frequency reading norms as an assessment tool for reading teachers. They felt that everyone associated with schools today needs to be aware of the increasing requirements for number- or data-driven student performance accountability. They go on to examine the use of assessments in oral reading fluency and its various components.

Classroom Application

Accuracy in word decoding, automaticity in recognizing words, and appropriate use of prosody or meaningful oral expression are the pathway to comprehension. If these skills are mastered, the students limited intellectually or cognitive resources can be used for greater comprehension, which is the higher-order thinking goal of fluency. Rasinski (2006) takes issue with teaching these three skills separately and feels that this type of instruction requires precious extra time out of the instructional day. Second, he feels that some of the activities focus only on gains in reading rates or reading faster for the sake of just reading faster. He feels that classroom practice needs to unify accuracy, automaticity, and prosodic reading methods.

So where does that leave teachers? You might be able to clinically engage younger students in separate instructional activities to strengthen these elements of fluency, but you pay a price for it. Students lose their motivation and incentive as you take the comprehension and meaning out of reading. Repeated reading is a common strategy for increasing fluency. However, the older the student, the less likely this method will motivate him or her to read. Would you want to improve your reading rate and fluency by using a repeated reading strategy? I'm sure these isolated strategies would not be very motivating for adult literacy classes either. It's like doing basketball or soccer drills in isolation and never engaging in a motivating authentic game.

Rasinski makes some good suggestions for fluency instruction. It is best described as authentic instruction. He suggests engaging students in performing passages that combine all three instructional goals. Any type of performance requires repeated readings, practice, or rehearsal. If performance is the incentive to practice, then what kind of texts lend themselves to expressive oral performance? Many types of texts are important yet offer a limited number opportunities for expressive interpretations. As Rasinski points out, a number of specific types of texts are meant to be performed and can be considered easy to perform. Songs, poetry, lyrics, plays, scripts (theater, movie, TV), monologues, and other types of oral presentations work well for expressive oral reading and mastery of meaning. This strategy exposes students to a wider range of reading material and also motivates students to master the elements of fluency and comprehension.

Rasinski states his purpose was to reinforce the recommendations of Hudson's group that repeated reading be used as a key instructional strategy. He adds that reading should also be meaningful, motivating, and provide expressive oral potential. We should be looking for text and activities that bring these ideas together to keep reading motivating and important in the students' lives.

Precautions and Possible Pitfalls

As with any type of performance, a teacher has to create a safe environment and a trusting relationship with his or her students. Many students with reading problems simply won't want to risk the social consequences of a public performance. While Rasinski touted the success of reading performance as an instructional tool, he failed to talk about the social factors involved in this type of activity. An empathetic teacher will need to use all his or her skills to build an environment where students are willing to take very personal risks.

Sources

Hasbrouck, J., & Tindal, G. A. (2006). Oral reading fluency norms: A valuable assessment tool for reading teachers. *The Reading Teacher, 59*(7), 636–644.

Hudson, R. F., Lane, H. B., & Pullen, P. C. (2005). Reading fluency assessment and instruction: What, why, and how? *The Reading Teacher, 58*(8), 702–714.

Rasinski, T. (2006). Reading fluency instruction: Moving beyond accuracy, automaticity, and prosody. *The Reading Teacher, 59*(7), 704–706.

5

Comprehension

Literacy is not a luxury, it is a right and a responsibility. If our world is to meet the challenges of the twenty-first century we must harness the energy and creativity of all our citizens.

—President Clinton on International
Literacy Day, September 8th, 1994

 Strategy 15: Try a "thinking out loud" strategy to help reveal children's thought processes as they try to make sense of text.

What the Research Says

 Think-alouds (thinking out loud strategy) remove the cloak of mystery surrounding the comprehension process as teachers and students verbalize their own thoughts while reading orally. Think-alouds require a reader to stop periodically, reflect on how a text is being processed and understood, and relate orally what reading strategies are being employed or not being employed. Research was conducted with fourth-grade students (Baumann, Jones, & Seifert-Kessell, 1992) to determine if thinking aloud strategies are an effective technique for helping students learn to monitor their comprehension.

Results from a series of quantitative assessments and in-depth, individual student interviews led researchers to the conclusion that think-aloud instruction was highly effective in helping students acquire a broad range of strategies (typical of highly effective readers) to enhance understanding of text and to deal with comprehension difficulties. Their research found that using think-alouds helped students develop an ability to monitor their reading comprehension and employ fix-up strategies when they detected comprehension difficulties. The researchers also recommend that students participate in the social construction of think-alouds, either as part of the lessons or within lessons.

Classroom Applications

As the phrase implies, "thinking out loud" is a great strategy to use to slow down the reading process and let students get a good look and feel for how skilled readers construct meaning from a text. Thinking aloud by the teacher and more capable students provides novice learners with a way to observe "expert thinking" usually hidden from the student. Many of us developed our skills as readers implicitly, by simply doing a lot of reading of all sorts of texts; after all, reading is a passion for us. Therefore, when we teach reading at the primary and secondary levels, we must take what we know and do *implicitly* and make it *explicit* for students, especially for struggling readers. Teachers and students use the think out loud strategy to monitor and improve comprehension and share the secrets of reading for meaning and understanding. Teachers can model aloud and think out loud to explain the strategies they use as they read. Students think out loud to show each other how to understand what is read.

Below is a beginning list of what skilled readers do implicitly; we need to help our students learn and apply these skills and strategies on a regular basis to improve their interactions with text.

Explore a Student's Prior Knowledge

Whenever effective readers approach new media, text, or other information, they consciously (or unconsciously) summon any information or background they have to relate to the topic, idea, people/characters, setting, historical context, author, similar events, and so forth. This process provides a foundation for the reading; it helps us to make sense of the new text.

Develop Goals and Objectives for Reading

Establishing what they expect to get out of the reading is another step common for skilled readers. Depending on the purpose, skilled readers adjust their reading to meet the chosen goal. Making students cognitive of the reason, purpose, or goal for the reading is a crucial initial step in helping them successfully interact with the text. Knowing why they are reading is the first step.

Decode Text Into Meanings and Words

These are the basic reading skills that our children *begin* to learn at the elementary level; but secondary teachers must continue to work on them as the texts and multimedia become more varied and sophisticated. Decoding text into words and meaning can also involve using strategies to define unfamiliar words using context clues or word parts (e.g., prefixes, suffixes, roots).

Identify, Engage, and Connect With the Text and Its Context

As skilled and effective readers move through a text and multimedia they constantly compare and contrast their knowledge and experience with what is presented and revealed in the text. This process of personal reflection on the text improves the reader's comprehension and understanding. Skillful readers often ask themselves (consciously or unconsciously) the following questions as they read: How is this like or unlike something I know or have experienced? How can I relate the ideas here to other texts I have read? How is this text (and the ideas presented in it) useful or relevant to me?

Engage Intellectually and Make Predictions

From the moment skilled readers pick up a text, they start making predictions about it. They look at all the parts of the text, the title, table of contents, dedication, number of pages, font size, photographs, commentary on the back or book jacket, and so on; and they begin to engage in making predictions regarding the text. As their reading progresses, they continue to alter their view in response to new information.

Visualize What You Read

One of the most powerful tools that skilled readers develop is their ability to imagine and visualize what they are reading. Mental pictures and intellectual role playing create the setting, visions of what the characters look like, in short, visually immerse the reader in the world of the story. In an abstract nonfiction text, the reader may create a mindset that helps him or her to keep track of the information and organize it.

Engage in Self Questioning and Mental Exploration and Challenges

Good readers view the writer as the other half of a good conversation. They make a habit of asking all types of questions as they react to the reading. They question the text, the writer, their own responses, the opinions, and other reactions to the reading. These may be questions that probe for a deeper understanding, or simply questions that voice their internal confusion and need for clarity. When explicitly taught, this is a skill that often shocks some of your less skilled readers; they often think it is time to stop reading when they are frustrated or confused, assuming that good readers rarely have these problems. It is a great lesson to see others dig for understanding.

Monitor Understanding and Summarize

Seasoned readers collect significant points as they navigate the media. Along the way, they drop certain facts and mental constructs into memory that help them make sense of the text. If something doesn't make sense, they may decide to let it go hoping it will become clear later or pause and take a closer look. They may take a step back to clarify and understand before moving on.

Use or Apply What Has Been Read

Both during and after the reading, skillful readers are constantly asking themselves about how the information relates to their lives or how could it be used. This goes back to a reader's goals and objectives. When students are reading a text to fulfill the demands of a goal or objective, they may keep the demands of the objective in mind, considering how they will apply information from the text to complete an assigned task or fill other intellectual needs. Discovering how reading applies to our lives and how readers identify with the information is essential for engaging students in text and dialog. Students often need help discovering the ways to reflect on how the reading relates to them.

Precautions and Possible Pitfalls

It is very important to decide how to use this information and the strategy. The reading skill level of the class will determine how much of this strategy you want to use. If you have too many skilled readers, you will lose them with a simple or boring text.

On the other hand many times readers want to share and discuss their experiences reading a good book. Skilled readers usually like to exchange ideas regarding a provocative book or bit of text. Ultimately teachers will need to decide the role and nature of this strategy with each individual class.

Sources

Baumann, J. F., Jones, L. A., & Seifert-Kessell, N. (1993). Using think alouds to enhance children's comprehension monitoring abilities. *The Reading Teacher, 47*(3).

Sainbury, M. (2003). Thinking aloud: children's interactions with text. *Reading, Literacy and Language, 37*(3), 131–135.

Strategy 16: Use information trade book retellings to improve student comprehension of expository text structures.

What the Research Says

In the early literacy years, young children are mostly immersed in the narrative story genre, especially in the early elementary school years, and thus they generally find understanding expository texts, whether reading them or writing them, much more difficult than reading or writing stories. The most common expository text structures include description, sequence, comparison and contrast, cause and effect, and problem and solution, and teaching these text structures to young students can best facilitate reading and writing of exposition (Moss, 2004). Barbara Moss (2004) suggests that teachers can use information trade book retellings to teach students expository text structure. She maintains that information trade books are best suited for teaching expository text structures because they are well organized and clearly written. Retellings, Moss (2004) stresses, are not the same as summaries; rather, she says, retellings are oral or written postreading recalls during which children relate what they remember from reading a particular text, and when students retell, Moss (2004) says, they should recall as much of the information in the text as possible, and not just the main points as in a summary. Moss (2004) maintains that by retelling the expository text in information trade books, students can better understand text organization and identify relationships among pieces of information, not to mention developing their oral language abilities.

Classroom Applications

 Moss (2004) suggests that each text structure should be taught individually, first, because students will need time to master one structure before learning another and she suggests that sequence, comparison, and contrast may be easier for students to grasp and should be taught first, while description, cause and effect, and problem and solution are more challenging and should therefore come later in the sequence of instruction. Moss (2004, p. 714) suggests that teachers can use the following sequence for teaching expository text structures:

1. Introduce the organizational pattern.

2. Explain the pattern and when writers use it. Point out the signal words associated with the structure and share an example.

3. Model ways students can determine text structures when signal words are not used. The table of contents and headings can help in this area.

4. Introduce a graphic organizer for the pattern.

5. Read aloud a trade book or a section of a book illustrating the appropriate text structure. Ask students to listen for signal words that can help them identify the structure.

6. Using the overhead projector, involve the group in completing a graphic organizer illustrating the text type.

7. Ask students to work in pairs to locate examples of the structure in information trade books. They can search for examples of the signal words, as well as use headings and other text features to guide their search.

8. Have students diagram these structures using a graphic organizer.

Moss (2004) also suggests that a two-phase sequence can best facilitate student development of expository retelling skills: first, the teachers need to model the retelling process, followed by giving the students opportunities to practice retellings, and this can be done in small groups or pairs. At all times, students should be encouraged to make personal connections with the text.

Precautions and Possible Pitfalls

Because each text structure must be taught individually first, and because students will need time to master one structure, this method will be time-consuming for the reading teacher. Therefore, teachers must be committed to using this method for at least one semester so that their students will not be overloaded with too much too soon. In addition, information trade books must be selected with care so that they are interesting to the students.

Source

Moss, B. (2004). Teaching expository text structures through information trade book retellings. *The Reading Teacher, 57*(8), 710–717.

 Strategy 17: Explore these three ways to get students to interact with the text in reading classes: summarize, share insights, and question.

What the Research Says

 Reading is said to be an active rather than a passive process in which good readers actively monitor their reading process. Carrell (1998) observed that successful, strategic readers monitor their reading and state of learning, plan to use specific reading strategies, are not afraid to adjust appropriately and evaluate their efforts (whether they have been successful or not) after reading. Vicky Zygouris-Coe, Matthew Wiggins, and Lourdes Smith (2004) suggest that reading teachers can better engage their students with the text by following what they call a 3-2-1 strategy in which the students are first encouraged to summarize important points from text they are reading, then they share whatever insights they got on topics or any aspects of passages they found interesting, and this is followed by a questioning strategy giving students opportunities to ask questions about the text they have been reading. The goal of this 3-2-1 strategy is to maximize students' interaction with text, and they maintain that this strategy gets the students more involved with the text and encourages them to think independently by inviting them to become personally engaged in and with the text. This strategy can be used when students read a textbook, a novel, an article, or other instructional texts.

Classroom Applications

 Zygouris-Coe, Wiggins, and Smith (2004) suggest teachers model and provide opportunities for students to interact with text. The 3-2-1 strategy works as follows for any text or book: teachers first ask students to discuss three things they discovered after reading the text, then to discuss two interesting things they want to note as a result of reading the text, followed by asking one question they still have after reading the text. When discussing three things the students discovered, the teacher must first teach them summary skills, which he or she can do by getting them to summarize small sections of the text to make sure all are participating. A summary, of course, is a short, to-the-point outline of the main ideas in the text. When the students discuss two interesting things about the text they noted, teachers can encourage them to think about what they enjoyed most or what was most relevant to their everyday lives. The final step of the 3-2-1 strategy is to get students to write one question they still have about the text. This question can link the text to their everyday lives.

Precautions and Possible Pitfalls

 As noted previously, teachers must model this strategy to their students slowly and carefully before asking them to do it, because they must also teach their students how to summarize; thus, although this 3-2-1 strategy is useful, teachers should note that it may take some time before their students are comfortable using it, and they may have to model it several times. Obviously, teachers can use this strategy only after their students know how to summarize.

Sources

Carrell, P. L. (1998). Can reading strategies be successfully taught? *ARAL, 21*(1), 1–20.

Zygouris-Coe, V., Wiggins, M. B., & Smith, L. H. (2004). Engaging students with the text: The 3-2-1 strategy. *The Reading Teacher, 58*(4), 381–384.

 Strategy 18: Use drama techniques such as drawing, interviewing, and story theater in the class to help students interact with the text.

What the Research Says

Many literacy teachers assign one novel for the entire class to read so that they can determine how the class as a whole understands the text. However, it is sometimes difficult for teachers to try to coordinate how all the students will react to and interact with that text. Leorna Macy (2004) suggests that one way to get the class working together as a whole with an assigned novel is to have them experience the novel through drama. Macy (2004) maintains that when teachers use drama techniques to teach appreciation of novels, they allow their students to explore meanings way beyond the text itself, and this approach also allows the students to form their own (rather than teacher-approved) responses to the novel.

Macy (2004) explains her technique, which emphasizes interaction and, using Rosenblatt's (1978) transactional theory of reading as a backdrop, she defines interaction as that between the reader and the text as separate entities. The reader, according to Rosenblatt's transactional theory, draws on her or his own personal life experiences, which reflects the reader's cultural, social, and personal history as well as past experiences with language; when reading, the reader constructs meaning based on what is in the text and what is in the reader's mind. Macy (2004) noted that this meeting of reader and text results in the reader appreciating the aesthetics of the text when interacting with it and stirs the reader's personal feelings, ideas, and attitudes. Reading teachers who want to emphasize a novel's aesthetics can then use drama techniques including such activities as drawing, dancing, miming, talking, role-playing, writing, and oral interpretation.

Classroom Applications

Among the various drama techniques Macy (2004) suggests as classroom applications teachers can adapt, depending on their teaching situations, the following seem most useful: drawing, story theater, and interview. For drawing, Macy (2004) suggests using two drama strategies in the first lesson, imaging and collective drawing. First, students read information from the novel about the setting so that they can create an image of what they are reading. Next, the collective drawing strategy focuses on building a context, with students working in small groups or as a whole class to make a collective image of a place; the drawing eventually becomes a concrete reference for ideas that are discussed.

Another technique that Macy (2004) suggests is story theater, which includes giving witness, caption making, and voice in the head. In giving witness, students relate to others what is happening in the story, which not only helps them recall the story but also links attitudes to events in that story. Caption making, in which the students compose slogans and titles, prepares the students for story theater in which one person reads the story of the characters in the story, and groups of two or three read selected pieces of the text aloud to the whole class. At this stage of the drama adaptation, Macy (2004) also incorporates a "voice in the head" strategy, which encourages the students to reflect on what a character is thinking and feeling at a particular time in the story. For the interview stage of this process, students must formulate their own questions about the novel, and the teacher can also get them to suggest their own answers.

Precautions and Possible Pitfalls

Reading teachers who use drama techniques to help their students construct the meaning of a novel must be aware that the students' meanings may not be the same as the teachers' suggested "appropriate meanings"; teachers must therefore develop a strategy for dealing with such differences. In addition, drama techniques should not be used exclusively; reading teachers should still provide some general comprehension questions to make sure students do not forget how to answer such questions. In fact, Macy (2004) maintains that drama strategies should not always be used with a novel, possibly twice a week at most.

Sources

Macy, L. (2004). A novel study through drama. *The Reading Teacher, 5*(3), 240–248.
Rosenblatt, L. (1978). *The reader and the text, the poem: The transactional theory of literacy work.* Carbondale: Southern Illinois University Press.

Strategy 19: Allow students to choose what they want to read.

What the Research Says

Richard Day and Julian Bamford (2004) suggest the best results from an extensive reading program in schools come when students have freedom to select the materials they want to read rather than having a teacher select material. This way the students choose material they can expect to understand, enjoy, and even to learn from. Day and Bamford (2004) also boldly suggest that, if students choose what they want to read, we should also allow them to stop reading anything they find difficult or uninteresting, but only within the extensive reading program.

Classroom Applications

 One way of incorporating this freedom of choice system is to establish a class library. If you're setting up a library and want your students to read whatever they choose, one idea is to ask each student to bring one or two books to "donate" to the library, which they will read first. After a student has read his or her book, he or she can make a brief presentation to the class about its contents and why others should read it. Thus begins the exchange of books, with each original owner being responsible to keep account of who is reading his or her book; this also reduces the time the teacher spends monitoring this process. One way of starting this sharing is to begin each class with a three-minute reading by a class member who has finished a book.

Precautions and Possible Pitfalls

 Each teacher must monitor the materials to ensure they are appropriate for the grade level in terms of difficulty and subject matter without specifically censoring the reading materials.

Source

Day, R., & Bamford, J. (2004). *Extensive reading*. New York: Cambridge University Press.

 Strategy 20: Use paraphrasing to promote reading comprehension.

What the Research says

Candace Fisk and Beth Hurst (2003) maintain that, contrary to some opinions that the word *paraphrasing* implies students copying from encyclopedias, changing only a few words to write a report, the technique can be used to promote reading comprehension. This is because paraphrasing reinforces such reading skills as identifying the main idea and finding supporting details, while integrating such forms of communication as reading, writing, listening, and speaking. Therefore, Fisk and Hurst (2003) suggest that when teachers first introduce the concept of paraphrasing to students, they should clearly explain what it means and why it is useful in promoting reading comprehension. Students must be told that paraphrasing is a general rewriting in their own words that maintains the original meaning. Students must therefore be able to keep the voice of the original author (comical, serious, sarcastic), and this process helps readers identify characters in the reading.

Classroom Applications

 Fisk and Hurst (2003) offer the following four steps for using paraphrasing to promote reading comprehension: initial reading of text followed by discussion, second reading of text followed by note-taking, written paraphrasing, sharing of written paraphrase. First, the students read a text silently, and after vocabulary problems are clarified, they are asked to identify the main idea of the text. They can also be asked specific questions related to the text's tone and style. After they have became familiar with the main idea of the text, students read it again, this time looking for main ideas and supporting details but avoiding using the same vocabulary in the text. When they have finished taking notes, they turn in copies of the text they were reading, so they have to rely only on their own words but retaining the original voice in writing the paraphrase. Finally, when they have finished their paraphrase, students form pairs and share their stories by answering questions: How are the paraphrases similar? How are they different? How is the author's voice communicated in the two students' papers?

Precautions and Possible Pitfalls

Although Fisk and Hurst (2003) point out that paraphrasing can be used in upper elementary, middle, and high school, teachers should be cautious about using the technique before students are ready; it may overload their processing systems, because it involves all four modes of communication: reading, writing, speaking, and listening. Teachers must be aware of their students' developmental levels in reading before using paraphrasing, and when they do incorporate it, they should do so only along with other strategies to promote comprehension.

Source

Fisk, C., & Hurst, B. (2003). Paraphrasing for comprehension. *The Reading Teacher,* 57(2), 182–185.

Strategy 21: Develop critical thinking and reasoning ability through the use of fiction and nonfiction books in the content areas.

What the Research Says

Hopper's research (2005) considers the findings on teen reading based on data collected for one week in May 2002 from 707 school children between ages 11 and 15 in 30 schools in the southwest of England. The article reflects on the adolescent reading choices, influences on those choices, and the importance of profiling all reading experiences beyond books. This includes "new" literacies considered today such as Internet use, magazines, newspapers, comic books, and other areas not typically included in traditional literacy activities.

The study supports past research in that it found no significant decline in student literacy habits.

Foster (2006) draws from her personal classroom practices, involving popular mainstream literature in her science curriculum to foster critical thinking and reasoning skills. Text is carefully selected for its ability to challenge and promote intellectual exploration of how specific content information can be found in mainstream text. This information is used to promote authentic applications in critical thinking about and analysis of nontextbook information.

Classroom Applications

Go to any educational conference and you will always find a few content area presenters sharing their ideas and practices on the use of trade books and related material within a content area curriculum. Regina Foster, Alliance Coordinator at Oklahoma State University, presents a most compelling strategy at the National Science Teachers Association Conference for the use of trade books in various science class activities. Her literacy goal is engaging students' reasoning and critical thinking skills, coupled with science content, to explore selected trade books that meet her curricular expectations.

Following are a few of her book choices that have proved successful over time. Her list comes from a science perspective, but the overall idea can be applied in many content areas and with many age groups and literacy levels. Foster's picks are listed here to trigger ideas on the use of popular books, beyond the content textbook, to produce curriculum and activities:

- *Awakenings* by Dr. Oliver Sacks

  She uses this book in her anatomy/physiology classes. The focus is on the nervous system, chemicals and the brain, and the ethics and morals surrounding health care and health care professionals.

- *My Sister's Keeper* by Jodi Picoult

  This book takes a critical look at the ethics of a young girl's treatment for leukemia, the effects of chemotherapy, transfusions, and other organ transplants. It is used in biology classes to examine a family's relationships as it deals with a teenager's disease. In some cases, selected passages are copied and used independent of reading the entire book.

- *Harry Potter and the Sorcerer's Stone* by J. K. Rowlings
- *Bezoar Stones* by Corey Malcom

  These books are used in chemistry classes and focus on an examination of bezoar stones, their history, and their uses. Magic is also the focus of the Harry Potter series, but the books include lots of chemistry, too. The Harry Potter series has gotten recognition as a trade book that offers curricular teaching and learning opportunities.

- *Woman in the Mist* by Farley Mowat
- *Gorillas in the Mist* by Dian Fossey

  You can use selected portions of these books in environmental science and ecology units. They also deal with the political and cultural issues surrounding the science, and like some of the other books mentioned here, these books were translated into film.

- *The Lorax* by Dr. Seuss

  You migh expect *The Lorax* to be used in an elementary school context, but Foster uses it for high school activity. It, too, stresses environmental issues.

- *The War of the Worlds* by H. G. Wells
- *The War of the Worlds* transcripts, as performed by Orson Welles on the Columbia Broadcasting System, Sunday, October 30, 1938, from 8:00 to 9:00 P.M.

  These texts are used as prompts in general science classes. Classes examine the way science was used in a greater cultural and societal context. Was the science used accurately or used less accurately to enhance a fictional story?

- Foster also scans content journals and periodicals for readings on science topics.

  Hopper's research (2005) connects to Foster's idea in that a savvy teacher can explore popular teenage literature and look for books and other popular texts from which to extract activities and lesson plans.

Precautions and Possible Pitfalls

 Copyright law exists to protect the intellectual property of writers, artists, musicians, and other creative people who produce original works in many areas. Copyright law ensures the right of these groups of creative individuals to profit from their artistic efforts by requiring permission to use their work. The educational fair use guidelines are an important limitation of copyright law.

Detailed guidelines pertaining to educational fair use can be found in their entirety at http://fairuse.stanford.edu/.

Sources

Hopper, R. (2005). What are teenagers reading? Adolescent fiction reading habits and reading choices. *Literacy, 39*(3), 113–128.

Foster, R. (2006). *Reading science: A critical examination of both fiction and nonfiction material.* National Science Teachers Association Conference, Anaheim, California. April 6–9, 2006.

Strategy 22: Use talk as a strategy in the reading class.

What the Research Says

 Many students think that reading is a silent self-directed activity that is done alone. Carole King (2001) shows, however, that reading can also be a social activity, especially in a reading class where students have short attention spans and become restless if left to fend for themselves during scheduled "silent reading" periods. King (2001) suggests that adding a social dimension to reading can make reading periods more dynamic with the increased interaction among students and teacher as they help one another become better readers. King (2001) adds that the role of talk within the literature circle or group reading sessions can also help students develop their oral skills, because they learn how to communicate effectively as they express their ideas with one another. King (2001) also maintains that these group reading sessions can be an effective strategy to get the quieter students in class to speak up and contribute to classroom discussions. This is because small group discussions are not as intimidating as whole class discussions, and quieter students can thus slowly build up their self-confidence and self-esteem among smaller groups of peers. King (2001) emphasizes that reading teachers should develop an atmosphere where each student's contribution to the discussion is considered valuable because the group recognizes that there are no right or wrong answers.

Classroom Applications

Carole King (2001) suggests that teachers can make students better readers by making them conscious of their reading and their role as readers. One way of achieving this, she says, is by encouraging them to voice out their thoughts and feelings relating to the text they are reading, that is, verbalizing the "inner speech" that reading involves (p. 34). Talk, as used in class discussions, is now elevated to a teaching tool, making amorphous, unstructured talk, often frowned on in classrooms, "exploratory talk." King (2001) advises teachers to "value the tentative, hypothetical nature of text-related talk, for this enables participants to voice and clarify any confusions and questions, as well as thoughts they may not have realised they had" (p. 35). This is something worth thinking about especially for teachers and principals who believe such talk is unproductive and should be stifled.

King (2001) noted that teachers often neglect children's interest in pursuit of achieving our prescribed teaching objectives. However, for such exploratory talk to be useful in helping students to become better readers, it is important that students are "actively involved" in the text. This brings up the issue of students' interests and how teachers can find texts that will interest and engage them. Students themselves could recommend books, articles, or texts that they find interesting and would like the classroom to explore. From this list, teachers can choose texts they think are sufficiently challenging for the students as readers. Teachers can also make an effort to observe their students and listen in on them sometimes, to find out the kinds of issues they concerned about and their likes or dislikes. Teachers must also play an important role in student group discussions. They are crucial in guiding the conversations and encouraging students to speak up and contribute. However, King (2001) suggests that teachers have to be careful not to be overzealous facilitators and dominate the conversations with their own versions or perceptions of the story. It may be helpful for teachers to come up with their own set of questions and probing cues.

Precautions and Possible Pitfalls

Some of the possible problems with this kind of activity are the digressions to gossip that students are so fond of whenever they come together. It may be helpful, too, for students to come up with their own list of questions and to decide what they should ask or say in their group discussions. This list could be a joint effort of the class and teacher. Each student will then have a copy of the list to guide him or her in group discussions until the students are able to do it themselves and explore more difficult texts with their peers and gradually on their own.

Source

King, C. (2001). "I Like Group Reading Because We Can Share Ideas": The Role of Talk Within the Literature Circle. *Reading*, April 2001, 32–36.

 Strategy 23: Use scaffolding to improve reading comprehension.

What the Research Says

 Kathleen Clark and Michael Graves (2005) maintain that scaffolding plays a vital role in developing a student's reading comprehension. They define scaffolding as a temporary supportive structure teachers create to assist students in accomplishing a task they probably could not have completed alone, and it is grounded in Vygotsky's social constructivist view of learning in which a child's development first appears in collaboration with an adult. According to Clark and Graves, what makes scaffolding an effective teaching technique is that it helps keep a task whole, while students learn to understand and manage the individual parts, without being too overwhelmed with the whole.

Classroom Applications

Clark and Graves (2005) describe different types of scaffolding, such as moment-to-moment verbal scaffolding and instructional frameworks that foster content learning that may be useful for reading teachers. For *moment-to-moment verbal scaffolding,* the teacher prompts his or her students by asking probing questions. According to Clark and Graves, teachers must consider two things while scaffolding in such a manner: how their instructional talk moves students closer to the goal, and how they can use students' responses to make them more aware of the mental processes in which they are engaged. *Instructional frameworks that foster content learning* are used to guide and improve students' understanding as they read and may or may not include moment-to-moment verbal scaffolding. Here, teachers use the strategy of questioning the author. For example, Clark and Graves suggest that teachers could ask the following questions:

- What do you think the author means by that?
- How does that connect with what the author has already told us?
- How did the author work that out for us?
- Did the author explain it clearly?
- What's missing?
- What do we need to find out?

Precautions and Possible Pitfalls

 Teachers should be aware that, during the planning phase of scaffolding, they must consider all their students' strengths and weakness and who will be doing the reading, the reading selection itself, and the purpose of the reading. So it is important that the teacher create some prereading, during-reading, and postreading activities designed to assist this particular group of students reach those purposes; otherwise the activity may not be as effective as it could be. In addition, teachers should be able to provide enough support for students to succeed, but not so much that they do all the work—not an easy balance to maintain.

Source

Clark, K., & Graves, M. (2005). Scaffolding students' comprehension of text. *The Reading Teacher, 58*, 570–580.

 Strategy 24: Teach young children "radical change" characteristics in picture books.

What the Research Says

 Sylvia Pantaleo (2004) has suggested that Dresang and McClelland's (1999) concept of *radical change* can be used to help children appreciate and evaluate the types of changes in children's literature. According to Pantaleo, Dresang's radical change framework identified three types of change in literature for children: changing forms and formats (Type 1), changing perspectives (Type 2), and changing boundaries (Type 3). Type 1 incorporates one or more of the following characteristics: "graphics in new forms and formats, words and pictures reaching new levels of synergy, nonlinear organization and format, nonsequential organization and format, and multiple layers of meaning and interactive formats" (p. 178). Type 2 uses "multiple perspectives, visual and verbal, previously unheard voices and youth who speak for themselves" (p. 178). Type 3 has changing boundaries and includes "subjects previously hidden, settings previously overlooked, characters portrayed in new complex ways, new types of communities, and unresolved endings" (p. 178).

Classroom Applications

 Radical change characteristics require readers to make complex decisions about whether to continue with the "main" narrative or visual text or to pursue another textual or illustrative path. For example, *The Three Pigs* contains pictures within pictures and stories within stories, and there are multiple narratives in both text and illustrations. According to Pantaleo (2004), teachers can engage the class in interactive read-aloud sessions that ensure active student involvement while posing more "open" questions, to which multiple responses are required. Picture books with radical change characteristics demand a higher level of sophistication and complexity with respect to predicting, but according to Pantaleo (2004), these books can teach critical thinking skills, visual-literacy skills, and interpretative skills. Pantaleo (2004) offers the following as examples of picture books exhibiting radical change characteristics:

- Brett, J. (2002). *Who's that knocking on Christmas Eve?* New York: G. P. Putnam's Sons.
- Coy, J. (2003). *Two old potatoes and me.* New York: Knopf.

Precautions and Possible Pitfalls

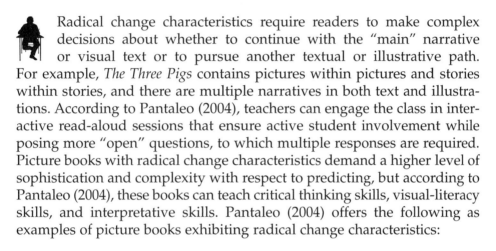 Because radical change characteristics require readers to make complex decisions about whether to continue with the "main" narrative or visual text or to pursue another textual path, teachers may need to spend a lot of time instructing readers exactly what to look for in these radical change books. Introducing radical change books may therefore be easier said than done.

Sources

Dresang, E. T., & McClelland, K. (1999). Radical change: Digital age literature and learning. *Theory into Practice, Vol. 38*(3), 160–167.

Pantaleo, S. (2004). Young children and radical change characteristics in picture books. *The Reading Teacher, 58*, 178–187.

6

Interventions for Struggling and At-Risk Readers

Not all readers are leaders, but all leaders are readers.

—Harry Truman

 Strategy 25: Don't wait for formal testing to begin interventions for students with reading disabilities.

What the Research Says

In a study of 40 first and second graders in Alabama, researchers looked for correlative findings on 20 students who were not referred (Sofie & Riccio, 2002). The students were assessed using formal and informal methods. For the formal assessment, researchers administered the WISC-III, the WJ-R (Letter-Word Identification, Passage Comprehension, and Word Attack); CTOPP was used for phonological awareness (segmenting, bending, and elision), and the Dyslexia Screening Instrument was used for the teacher rating. For the informal assessment, teachers used curricular-based assessments addressing a different aspect of reading skills; the results were compared and found to be highly correlative.

Given the controversies surrounding norm-referenced testing instruments (cultural bias leading to the disproportionate number of minority and English-language learner, or ELL students diagnosed with disabilities), curricular-based assessments yielded similar results and inspired teachers to begin interventions immediately. In addition, many of the quick in-class assessments can be used to check the efficacy of the interventions on an ongoing basis.

Classroom Applications

 Many teachers routinely use quick fluency assessments to gauge student placement on the reading continuum. These assessments can be just as effective in determining appropriate reading interventions for students. Some common examples are sight word lists and small group read-aloud sessions. By using and acting on the information gained in these informal assessments, teachers can begin to identify and remediate problem areas for students rather than wait for the child to be so far behind that he or she qualifies for special education services.

In higher grades, the gap between fluent readers and reluctant readers widens into a greater and greater achievement gap. Student performance on assignments early in the year will often lead teachers to identify which students would benefit from intervention strategies. Suggesting these strategies or inviting students to participate in support programs before they have failing grades or require a formal referral process may circumvent the need for alternative placement.

Precautions and Possible Pitfalls

Literacy interventions are effective in most cases, and certainly will not hinder a student's growth; teachers should not postpone a referral for a student who would benefit from special education services. Instead, they should initiate the referral process according to their site or district policy and then begin intervention strategies that they would normally employ. They should also keep track of what is working, to bring to the team meeting after the student has been formally assessed. One way to accomplished this is by keeping a portfolio of student work samples that highlight successes as well as areas for growth.

Source

Sofie, C. A., & Riccio, C. A. (2002). A comparison of multiple methods for the identification of children with reading disabilities. *Journal of Learning Disabilities,*
35(3), 234–245.

 Strategy 26: Use early literacy
intervention strategies to facilitate
appropriate student behavior.

What the Research Says

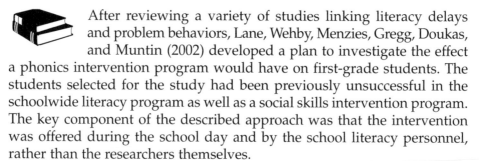 After reviewing a variety of studies linking literacy delays
and problem behaviors, Lane, Wehby, Menzies, Gregg, Doukas,
and Muntin (2002) developed a plan to investigate the effect
a phonics intervention program would have on first-grade students. The
students selected for the study had been previously unsuccessful in the
schoolwide literacy program as well as a social skills intervention program.
The key component of the described approach was that the intervention
was offered during the school day and by the school literacy personnel,
rather than the researchers themselves.

The results were dramatic, in that all of the students in the study
improved their attack skills. With the exception of one student, antisocial
behavior on the playground and the classroom decreased in all of the
participants. The implication the researchers noted was the importance of
beginning the literacy intervention as soon as possible, especially when
antisocial behavior has been noted.

Classroom Applications

Often teachers make the mistake of viewing behavior problems as
one issue and academic performance as another, unrelated issue.
Although it is common knowledge that frustration with an academic endeavor can produce an outburst of misbehavior in a student,
there is evidence that the link is stronger than just cause and effect.
Teachers can contribute to their student's success with literacy and social
behavior by noticing lack of performance and offering the appropriate
interventions as early as possible. Small group instruction in specific
reading strategies can contribute to positive student behavior. Students
who receive literacy support with phonics instruction and achieve success

in reading independently seem to be calmer and better behaved during class. Whether it is the individual attention of small group instruction, the intrinsic reward of succeeding at decoding, or the actual neural connections formed in the literate brain is unclear. What is clear is the need for additional assistance for struggling students as early as possible!

Precautions and Possible Pitfalls

 Caution should be taken not to assume that early literacy intervention will cure all misbehavior. Some students may have behavior disorders that need to be addressed by a psychologist. Although these students will still benefit from literacy support, phonics and reading strategy instruction may not be sufficient to meet their needs.

Source

Lane, K. L., Wehby, J. H., Menzies, H. M., Gregg, R. M., Doukas, G. L., & Muntin, S. M. (2002). Early literacy instruction for first-grade students at-risk for antisocial behavior. *Education and Treatment of Children, 25*(4), 438–459.

 Strategy 27: Consider consulting with the speech pathologists to create a multifaceted approach to build students' vocabulary and assist them in reading comprehension.

What the Research Says

 Johnson, Tulbert, Sebastian, Devries, and Gompert (2000) describe an inclusive classroom model in which the speech pathologists, special education teacher, and general education teacher collaborate on lesson planning and delivery for a vocabulary unit. Using a language-board approach, the three teachers selected the words that their fifth-grade students would need to comprehend a specific story, taking into account the specific goals of the students receiving special services. The result was a vocabulary lesson that included the following instructional approaches:

Mnemonic keyword—structuring a similar sounding word to key into the original word.

Interactive process—students design their own memory clues and images about the word.

Rehearsal—students hear the definition of a word and then repeat it.

Holistic instruction—students learn about syntax, morphology, semantics, and pragmatics for a given word.

Paired oral and written language—students use the words (reading, writing, listening, and speaking).

Classroom Applications

Students demonstrate a wide range of vocabulary development in any classroom, but even more so when they have learning disabilities. Issues with auditory processing and short- and long-term memory can adversely affect their reading comprehension. Many teachers will prepare students for unfamiliar vocabulary with a word list and definitions. Although this technique is popular and many textbooks include word lists, students aren't always able to internalize these words at a level where they aid comprehension, especially in other contexts.

Using the expertise of speech pathologists can help teachers develop a multifaceted approach to vocabulary instruction. Understanding word origins and morphology can assist students in their long-range understanding of language as well as give them the tools they need to decode unfamiliar words. By combining this approach with student-created mnemonics as well as formal definitions, students demonstrate increased comprehension.

Precautions and Possible Pitfalls

Teachers need to be wary of requiring students to learn long lists of vocabulary without any context. Test results may be good, but the meanings are quickly lost when the words are not put in the context of authentic speech, writing, or reading. Don't let the test results give you a false sense of security.

Source

Johnston, S. S., Tulbert, B. L., Sebastian, J. P., Devries, K., & Gompert, A. (2000). Vocabulary development: A collaboration effort for teaching content. *Intervention in School & Clinic, 35*(5), 311–316.

Strategy 28: Consider peer tutoring, especially cross-age tutoring, as an appropriate intervention for students whose struggle to read continues to be significantly below grade level.

What the Research Says

Two studies (Fisher, 2001; Van Keer & Verhaeghe, 2005) looked at various aspects of peer tutoring, both same-age and cross-age, as vehicles for reading instruction.

Fisher's work compared instructional outcomes of two groups of "less proficient" readers in a typical remedial middle school reading class. One sample group of 22 students participated in tutor training and the cross-age tutoring of first and second graders, while another group of 23 students were not provided the peer tutoring opportunity. In this research, cross-age tutoring meant older students, under a teacher's guidance, helping one or more younger student(s) learn or practice a skill or concept. This provided the older learners with an authentic reason for practicing and improving their reading performance and competence.

The elementary school that provided the tutoring opportunities for their students served as a feeder school for both middle schools in the study. All schools in this study were considered "inner city" in terms of ethnic diversity, number of languages spoken by students, and socioeconomic level. Both middle school classes used the same texts, and throughout the year more difficult texts were added as both the tutors and tutees continued to develop their literacy skills. The teacher of the experimental cross-age class developed lesson plans for the peer tutors to use. Lesson plans were then modeled and practice time was given before the young tutors met with their younger tutees.

The literacy development of the middle school students was assessed in a number of ways. Data on reading comprehension was gathered by and from the schoolwide assessment system, the Gates-MacGinite Reading Tests, fourth edition, and the Stanford Achievement Test (SAT-9). In addition, classroom behaviors were observed approximately three times a week. The two groups were compared and contrasted.

The literacy-related instructional outcomes for the tutors presented significant increases or growth, and students who tutored outperformed the comparison group of students in both vocabulary and comprehension on both testing measures.

Classroom observations showed student tutors reading increasingly difficult texts at increased speed and fluency. The tutors also demonstrated their understanding of rhythm, rhyme, stress, and intonation as they modeled skills for their tutees. In addition, the tutor group exhibited progress in writing in their weekly journals.

In addition to Fisher's 2001 work, Van Keer and Verhaeghe (2005) compared and contrasted same-age and cross-age tutoring and found that cross-age tutoring seemed to create better instructional environments for both the tutor and the tutee. Tutors became better readers and better tutors. It should also be noted that those involved in cross-age tutoring were significantly less worried about negative self-efficacy–related thoughts than those involved in same-age peer tutoring.

Classroom Applications

If you are looking for working models and supporting evidence for the effectiveness of peer tutoring, you need look no further than drug and alcohol abuse and prevention for an effective peer resource model. Successful relationships within these models have been noted for many years. In addition to instructional goals and content knowledge, peer relationships contribute to social and cognitive development as students relate to each other and work together in cooperative and collaborative ways.

Classroom cross-age tutoring has many definitions. In a pure state, it is simply one child/student instructing another in material in which the first student is an "expert" and the other student is a "novice." In reality, not all tutors are experts. Some are randomly assigned, some with training, others with little or absolutely no training. To complicate matters, cross-age tutoring or any type of same-age or peer tutoring in reading also includes teaching and developing social behaviors, classroom discipline, and enhancing peer relationships. These types of relationships also delve into self-esteem. Some writers cite wider benefits as well, such as motivating potential teachers and developing skills transferable to parenting.

The drug and alcohol prevention model has a track record of positive results. In the introductions to both of the cited papers, the researchers describe positive results from other research studies on low-achieving and other high-need students who benefit from tutor training and tutor-tutee activity. They also discuss greater academic achievement, more control, higher self-esteem, improved social skills, better attitudes toward school, and lower rates of dropout, truancy, and tardiness with involvement in some form of peer tutoring. Tutees were also found to receive academic benefits and growth in addition to some of the intangibles identified with tutor benefits.

Why does peer tutoring work? Many believe tutors and tutees speak a little more of the same "language" regarding school academics. They are closer to the same knowledge level and status. Also, tutors may simply be good teachers. Prompting and guiding, praise, attention, and encouragement may be natural parts of the tutor's personality. Key to success is the relevant help the tutor gives, which is

- appropriately elaborated;
- timely and within the instructional curricular context;
- understandable to the targeted student(s);
- facilitates the tutee really using the new information; and
- is authentically taken advantage of by the tutee.

Assessment and evaluation are a little more difficult to gauge than the more teacher-centered instructional outcomes. However, the total language competence—speaking, writing, and reading—is hard to measure anyway. Teachers can observe and interact with their students during tutorial and writing sessions and profile changes in reading, talking, writing, and social responsibility for learning.

Finally, cross-age tutoring works well after it has been established for a period of time. If you start a program, expect growing pains until the program has been established for a while.

Need help? Try these sites:

Gaustad, 1992 at http://www.nwrel.org/

The Resource Center: Tools and Training for Volunteer and Service Programs

Reading Helpers: A Hand Book for Training Community Partners at http://www.nationalserviceresources.org/

Topping, 1988: The Peer Tutoring Handbook at http://www.nwrel.org/

Precautions and Possible Pitfalls

 Neither study offered much insight regarding potential problems. However, it is safe to say that not every student exhibits the maturity and responsibility necessary to work as a tutor or a tutee. You may want to consider a performance contract for potential tutors that could take the form of a rubric for your behavior expectations and consequences.

From a more negative perspective, resistance to peer tutoring comes from the notion and tradition that knowledge is best transferred from adult to child (teacher to student). In addition, teachers and others often see peer tutoring as "messy" or just another layer of instruction hindering knowledge transfer. Also some parents resistant peer relationships because they view their son or daughter at an educational disadvantage in these relationships and prefer the teacher interact with their student.

This is especially true when high-achieving students are asked to tutor low-achieving students.

Many educators see the low and medium achievers as benefiting the most from peer tutor relationships. Parents of high achievers sometimes see this as a waste of their student's time. If you are considering tutoring relationships, it is very important to consider parent resistance. Educating parents and keeping them in the loop is important from a public relations point of view.

Sources

Fisher, D. (2001). Cross-age tutoring: Alternatives to reading resource room for struggling adolescent readers. *Journal of Instructional Psychology, 28*(4), 234–240.

Van Keer, H., & Verhaeghe, J. P. (2005). Effects of explicit reading strategies instruction and peer tutoring on second and fifth graders' reading comprehension and self-efficacy perceptions. *The Journal of Experimental Education, 73*(4), 291–329.

 Strategy 29: Make it routine practice to foster self-efficacy and motivation in your young readers.

What the Research Says

 Walker (2003) summarizes the major points of other authors and researchers since 1990 regarding the concepts of self-efficacy and the steps teachers can take to promote it in the teaching and learning environment. She then proposes and defines responses teachers can choose to increase self-efficacy, which in turn increases performance in reading and writing Her premise is that understanding students' motivation, particularly those exhibiting self-efficacy, can help educators better engage students in literacy activities, because young people who are efficacious are more likely to work hard, to persist, and to seek help to complete challenging tasks they sometimes believe are beyond their ability.

Classroom Applications

 Efficacious students do achieve and exhibit a group of attributes that make our teaching efforts rewarding. Self-efficacy refers to people's belief in their capabilities to carry out actions required to reach a high level of achievement. This success motivates the students to engage in more literacy activities, which in turn increases their reading and writing performance. Even when teachers know all this, they often fail to engage students in appropriate literacy activities that foster self-efficacy. It's no secret that the basic approach is to plan and provide interesting topics and clever activities to motivate students. However, motivation in self-efficacy is complex and difficult to nail down for curricular purposes. It is not easy for students to assess their own progress and achievement regarding self-efficacy in reading comprehension and writing.

Individuals develop their academic self-efficacy in a number of ways. Most commonly, successful learning experiences that are somewhat challenging yet doable create a sense of accomplishment that may significantly foster self-efficacy. Second, a strong source of self-efficacy is positive verbal response from parents, teachers, or peers that convey the student's capacity for performing literary activities. Related to this is accurate positive self-attributions developed by providing task-specific comments on student success and attributing that success to tasks that are learnable within the school environment. It is also helpful to reinforce the use of a variety of strategies to solve problems and work through activities. When faced with challenging activities, students with high self-efficacy apply metacognitive skills and strategies by asking themselves questions about concepts and content while checking their understanding.

Cultivating self-efficacy within a curricular framework is difficult. A number of authors have suggested that self-efficacy can be cultivated in low-performing students. Following are five suggestions mentioned most frequently:

- Giving students choice within activities.
- Encouraging strategic thinking about activities.
- Providing opportunities and tools for self-assessment.
- Changing the assessment purpose and context.
- Incorporating choice that asks students to make decisions about their interests and what they may already know about a task. When given a choice, students bring more effort to activities. Allowing choice in literacy activities increases motivation and authentic engagement. Teachers can provide a choice of activities within the day-to-day educational environment by offering personal reading and writing time, inquiry-oriented activities, and collaborative discussions based on student interests.

Many less than successful students look at failure and success differently than their more successful counterparts. In their eyes, success and failure are products of factors beyond their control. Luck, the teacher's attitude toward them, and the difficulty of the material have more influence on outcome and products of learning than their own ability and effort.

Often they do not recognize or acknowledge the effective strategies they use. Their mistakes are looked on as a continuous or repeated stream of blunders that have little value for learning. Learning from failure is rarely an option for them; failure just reinforces a negative self-image. They read and write without using or learning alternative strategies. What they are really saying is "I don't have strategies and I don't know how to do it."

Because of these phenomena, teachers need to teach reading and writing strategies such as monitoring of meaning and understanding and elaboration. Teachers can help students deal with mistakes and use alternative strategies when students confront difficult or challenging curriculum. Selected strategies can be modeled by the instructor, and student strategies can be defined and recognized as legitimate coping strategies. Low-efficacious students need this type of help.

Related to how failure and success work in the lives of low-efficacious students is the notion of self-assessment. Many low-performing and/or low-efficacious students believe they are not up to doing many tasks; therefore, they assess their work and abilities negatively. Literary progress is very difficult for students to assess. Positive self-evaluation and assessment raise self-efficacy because students understand the complex relationships between performance and their strategy and the literary processes.

Teacher-produced rubrics and checklists emphasizing the strategic steps within tasks help support effective adoption of strategies. Specific checklists help students revisit and rethink their strategic actions and help students see clearly the connections between strategy and personal success. Defining and quantifying the steps in strategies and showing their connections to success cultivate self-efficacy and empower students. These assessment tools help students attribute their success to strategic actions. Checklists also allow students to evaluate how their literacy and strategies are progressing. The checklist and rubric strategy work well in both reading and writing activities.

Grades and learning are supposed to go hand in hand, yet grades today often create a sense of false security for teachers, students, and parents. Students often believe grades equate to learning. Rather than focusing on grades, low-efficacious students should be focusing on what they are learning and what they can do. Changing the assessment context supports a learning notion rather than a performance orientation. Both specifically designed portfolios, with carefully crafted requirements, and student-led conferences with parents and teachers can become learner- rather than grade-centered assessment strategies.

Within a portfolio, students can evaluate their success with instructional activities and also help measure progress over time. Parents, students, and teachers can collaboratively review the students' work and what students can do. This all shifts the goals of assessment and evaluation from grade performance to specific learning goals that empower students and hopefully increase student efficacy. Past tasks are used to measure what students are learning, not to get better grades. Focus is on what they can do and how they are achieving their literacy goals.

By giving choices, learning literacy strategies provide self-assessment strategies, and changing the focus of assessment teachers can help guide students through more positive learning environments within more rigorous curriculum. All this contributes to increased ownership of learning, authentic engagement, and motivation/effort to continue to read and write, in turn enhancing self-efficacy.

Precautions and Possible Pitfalls

Self-efficacy is another element to consider when designing curriculum, assessment, and instructional strategies—and it does take time and add another layer of complexity. It's one of those educational intangibles that can't be measured, yet it is one of the most important characteristics a teacher can enhance. Nothing is more satisfying than having a room full of empowered students! Please consider it a necessity during curricular development and not just another required mandate. Self-efficacy is a gift you can help your students open.

Source

Walker, B. J. (2003). The cultivation of student self-efficacy in reading and writing. *Reading and Writing Quarterly, 19*, 173–187.

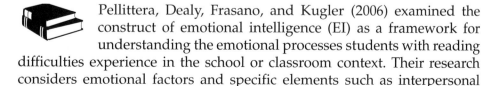

Strategy 30: Remember deficits in reading ability are often associated with a complex range of issues beyond academic achievement, such as lack of motivation, poor self-esteem, and difficult social settings.

What the Research Says

Pellittera, Dealy, Frasano, and Kugler (2006) examined the construct of emotional intelligence (EI) as a framework for understanding the emotional processes students with reading difficulties experience in the school or classroom context. Their research considers emotional factors and specific elements such as interpersonal interactions of peer groups, opportunities for developing emotional learning, and the dynamic affective-aesthetic responses of the individual students during the reading process. The article examines the underlying affective processes as they relate to cognition, motivation, and social functioning.

The authors state that a student's social and academic difficulties can be explained by the breakdown of these emotional processes. Students can experience difficulties in understanding social interaction with peers because of poor perception of emotional cues and failing to access emotional knowledge in school social situations. These factors affect performance in literacy instruction. Further, the authors state that constructs related to emotional intelligence examined in reading disability literature are understood to impact a student's academic functioning.

From a human ecological perspective, they describe the particular social-emotional and learning needs of students with reading disabilities that must be considered in creating an optimal personal learning environment fit. The authors list the systems that most directly impact the emotional dimensions of the student with reading disabilities:

- the psychological environment of the school and the classroom;
- the policies that determine the student's class placement, curriculum, and activities; and
- the structure of the student's interpersonal peer relations.

In their introduction, Pellittera, Dealy, Frasano, and Kugler (2006) describe the research of Gredler (1997), who stated that "individuals tend to interpret stress reactions and tension as indicators of vulnerability to performance. . . . Therefore the only way to alter personal efficacy is to reduce stress and negative emotional tendencies (during a difficult task)" (p. 290). They also list specific emotionally intelligent interventions and discuss their implementation in the school environment.

Classroom Applications

The overall culture of the school and the classroom can produce an environment that is so emotionally stressful that certain students become emotionally paralyzed or so academically dysfunctional that achievement is the last thing they want to strive for. Their behavior turns inward, often aimed at protecting their self-esteem, managing tensions within the learning or teaching environment, and/or coping with the frustration of academic cognitive tasks. Many students with reading problems have experienced excessive failure and have negative reactions and emotions connected to academic triggers and the teacher's instructional efforts in the school setting.

A major goal of intervention regarding these factors is to create an emotionally positive classroom environment that reduces the students' general anxieties and increases their positive associations with the school and classroom. The emotional environment of the school and the classroom are created by the interpersonal interactions between students and the adults within the setting. Teachers need to develop emotional awareness in themselves and begin to create a more intelligent classroom environment. Smiles, a pleasant tone of voice, and the use of encouraging words are a beginning. Removing negative stresses should be a curricular priority.

On a different level, a more systemic intervention considers the emotional needs of the students when scheduling classes and class activities. In some counseling situations, placement of students can include selecting educational environments that buffer threats to self-esteem and foster a student's willingness to take risks. Teacher matching can also be considered. Teachers have a responsibility to set and monitor group dynamics and the emotional tone of the classroom interactions. When a teacher values empathy, emotional sensitivity, and self-awareness in a learning environment, he or she can alter peer group dynamics and derogatory behavior within a classroom. Peer rejection and a student's failure at social adjustments are associated with academic performance within literacy strategies.

In addition, peer or cross-age tutoring arrangements pairing older struggling readers with younger struggling readers often set up a positive dynamic for both participants. With preparation, such arrangements provide a sense of competence for the older student that improve self-esteem, self-efficacy, and a positive emotional experience regarding reading.

Individually, the written text needs to become a source of motivation to read and a positive stimulus with positive affective associations. This is the big goal. Teachers need to help students become comfortable with not knowing all the words rather than experiencing reading mistakes as a sign that they are always wrong. Teachers also need to structure activities that are challenging yet still provide students with positive and successful experiences. From an emotional intelligence perspective, teachers can use reader-response activities to help the students examine their own emotions and develop the ability to reflect on their own responses to learning activities. In this way reading sessions can be used as a vehicle for personal social insight and self-awareness. Further, deciphering the text provides teaching and learning opportunities for young readers to begin to see themselves and their beliefs and feelings more clearly.

Planning for the emotion dynamics of the learning environment is essential. The emotional realm affects and influences the learning environment of struggling readers and learners in general. By becoming aware of and regulating the emotional reactions of students in literacy activities, teachers can increase not only fluency and mechanics but also the motivation to engage reading materials both inside and outside the classroom. You just have to remember that every academic task has an emotional component.

Precautions and Possible Pitfalls

It's not unusual to find that underachieving older students are resistant to strategies you might employ. A few students have had so many negative experiences and interactions with teachers and peers, school has become a painful place. The many attempts teachers have made to "reach" them over the years may have hardened them. Chances are, many teachers have tried to reach out to them and now they anticipate your efforts and are ready to resist. There are no easy answers for dealing with these students. Sometimes time and sincerity are the most effective qualities in building trust.

Sources

Gredler, M. E. (1997). *Learning and instruction: Theory into practice* (3rd ed.). Upper Saddle River, NJ: Merrill.

Pellittera, J., Dealy, M., Frasano, C., & Kugler, J. (2006). Emotionally intelligent interventions for students with reading disabilities. *Reading & Writing Quarterly, 22,* 155–171.

Strategy 31: Examine the effects of reading interventions on social outcomes for struggling elementary school readers.

What the Research Says

The purpose of the research by Pellittera, Dealy, Frasano, and Kugler (2006) and Wanzek, Vaugh, Kim, and Cavanaugh (2006) was to examine the effects of reading interventions on various aspects of social and emotional outcomes for both middle school students and elementary students. Their research focus may be different— one looks at reading outcomes first and the other at social outcomes— however, they both examine how educational strategies affect social and emotional function and well-being in groups of struggling readers in both middle school and elementary school.

Pellittera, Dealy, Frasano, and Kugler (2006) examined the construct of emotional intelligence (EI) as a framework for understanding the emotional processes students with reading difficulties experience in the school or classroom context. Their research considers emotional factors and specific elements such as interpersonal interactions in peer groups, opportunities for the development of emotional learning and the dynamic affective-aesthetic responses of the individual students during the reading process. The article examines the underlying affective processes as they relate to cognition, motivation, and social functioning.

Wanzek, Vaugh, Kim, and Cavanaugh (2006) selected social outcome effects as a primary goal in group reading interventions for struggling readers rather than reading outcomes. Overall, they found some evidence that social outcomes are positively associated with reading interventions. The majority of indicators in the cited studies support the notion that most interventions report positive social outcomes.

Classroom Applications

 Based on the research, the opportunity for students to work with their peers, as provided by group cooperative interactive learning, appears to have a positive effect on students' social and emotional outcomes. This suggests that teachers seeking practices to enhance social and emotional outcomes as well as reading outcomes may want to incorporate some tested types of group cooperative and interactive learning. Some teachers bring social and emotional interventions into their classrooms that specifically target these realms. Wanzek, Vaugh, Kim, and Cavanaugh (2006) took this a step further, combining both reading and literacy goals and social and emotional goals. They contrasted and compared four intervention types, exploring each intervention through a literature search. Relevant research was examined, and cumulative effects for each intervention were presented.

Group Interactive Learning

Group interactive learning includes interventions in which students are responsible for leading all or part of the lessons in a small group with other students. This includes cooperative learning and reciprocal teaching. In the research cited, these cooperative groups had a mix of student ability levels.

Wanzek, Vaugh, Kim, and Cavanaugh (2006) found group interactive learning was associated with yielding positive social outcomes. This suggests that teachers seeking instructional practices to enhance social outcomes as well as reading outcomes in their classrooms may want to incorporate the practice of group interactive learning.

Cross-Age and Peer Tutoring

Cross-age and peer tutoring are a bit different. Students work in pairs with one or both serving as a tutor; however, cross-age tutoring may be problematic if the tutor is the younger student.

Wanzek, Vaugh, Kim, and Cavanaugh (2006) looked at five studies on social outcome for students with reading deficits. Peer tutoring was not associated with improved social outcomes in the five studies examined.

However, in addition to the work of Wanzek, Vaugh, Kim, and Cavanaugh (2006), Van Keer and Verhaeghe (2005) compared and contrasted same-age and cross-age tutoring and found that cross-age tutoring seemed to create better instructional environments for both the tutor and the tutee. Tutors became better readers and better tutors. It should also be noted that those involved in cross-age tutoring were significantly less worried about negative self-efficacy–related thoughts than those involved in same-age peer tutoring.

Group Remedial Tutoring

In group remedial tutoring teachers provide reading instruction for struggling readers to more than one student at a time. This could include both small-group and whole-class instruction.

Six studies were examined by Wanzek, Vaugh, Kim, and Cavanaugh (2006). In general, they found studies with small groups showed positive gains on social outcomes from pretest to post-tests. One study noted moderate decreases in inappropriate behavior.

One-on-One Remedial Reading

One-on-one reading intervention is instruction for students struggling with reading provided by one teacher, parent, or student to only one student. This includes Reading Recovery, reading skill instruction, guided oral reading, and strategy reading instruction.

Wanzek, Vaugh, Kim, and Cavanaugh (2006) examined seven studies on one-on-one reading instruction for students with reading problems. Five of these reported overall positive effects on social outcomes.

Looking at the overall results of these interventions on social outcomes, though there are several caveats about interpretation, we can see some patterns of positive effects from reading interventions. While most readers are looking for positive literacy outcomes, it is refreshing to know that structured correctly, these interventions for struggling readers also can yield positive social outcomes! The interventions do double duty, filling two instructional goals at once!

Precautions and Possible Pitfalls

As with our other strategies on peer or group relationships as instructional strategies, these studies do not offer much insight regarding potential problems. So, like the other strategies, it is safe to say that not every student exhibits the maturity and responsibility necessary to work as a tutor or a tutee or perform in group settings. You may want to consider a performance contract for potential tutors that could take the form of a rubric for your behavior expectations and consequences. You also need to "teach" the activities and the appropriate behavior required to maximize the potential of the intervention.

From more negative perspectives, resistance to peer tutoring comes from the notion and tradition that knowledge is best transferred from adult to child (teacher to student). In addition, teachers and others often see peer tutoring as "messy" or just another layer of instruction hindering knowledge transfer. Also some parents are resistance to peer relationships because they view their son or daughter at an educational disadvantage in these relationships and prefer the teacher interact with their student. This is especially true when asking high achieving students to tutor low achieving students.

Many researchers see the low and medium achievers benefiting the most from peer tutor relationships. Parents of high achievers sometimes see this as a waste of their student's time. If you are considering tutoring relationships, it is very important to consider parent resistance. Educating parents and keeping them in the loop is important from a public relations point of view.

Sources

Pellittera, J., Dealy, M., Frasano, C., & Kugler, J. (2006). Emotionally intelligent interventions for students with reading disabilities. *Reading & Writing Quarterly, 22,* 155–171.

Van Keer, H., & Verhaeghe, J. P. (2005). Effects of explicit reading strategies instruction and peer tutoring on second and fifth graders' reading comprehension and self-efficacy perceptions. *The Journal of Experimental Education, 73*(4), 291–329.

Wanzek, J., Vaugh, S., Kim, A., & Cavanaugh, C. (2006). The effects of reading interventions on social outcomes for elementary students with reading difficulties: A synthesis. *Reading & Writing Quarterly, 22,* 121–138.

Strategy 32: Be patient with "slower learners" who require more reading practice than other students.

What the Research Says

Kathleen and Robert Cooter (2004) maintain that, although the term *slow learners* (IQ between 70 and 85) may be politically incorrect, some learners nevertheless function at a cognitive level that is significantly below their grade level in certain school tasks such as reading; hence they are "slower" than other learners and as such at a disadvantage. This problem is further compounded when these slower learners are not be identified until they reach grade school, so they may not have had any systematic early intervention to enhance their reading skills. However, Kathleen and Robert Cooter (2004) say all is not lost; some hopeful signs may be on the horizon, especially if literacy teachers take the positive attitude that slower learners do in fact learn when the reading materials they are presented are used at their appropriate level of learning.

Classroom Applications

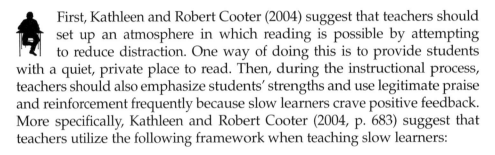 First, Kathleen and Robert Cooter (2004) suggest that teachers should set up an atmosphere in which reading is possible by attempting to reduce distraction. One way of doing this is to provide students with a quiet, private place to read. Then, during the instructional process, teachers should also emphasize students' strengths and use legitimate praise and reinforcement frequently because slow learners crave positive feedback. More specifically, Kathleen and Robert Cooter (2004, p. 683) suggest that teachers utilize the following framework when teaching slow learners:

1. Make the reading lessons short, using several short periods rather than one long one.

2. Add variety to the academic routine, such as games and puzzles.

3. Work on material that is somewhat challenging but also allows success. For this to be achieved, a process of ongoing assessment may be necessary to help teachers keep students within their learning range. Encourage parents to talk to their child to build language and vocabulary. For this, parents will need to be coached how to ask, for example, about their child's day at school in order to develop the child's language skills.

4. Include an amount of repetition in instruction. This is because slow learners need to overlearn various reading strategies and skills.

5. Provide meaningful, concrete activities rather than abstract ones. Have students continuously make cognitive connections to what they already know by engaging in concrete activities.

6. Give short, specific directions and have students repeat them.

7. The teacher should read in front of the students in order to set a good example.

8. Use a buddy reading system whenever possible because struggling readers can often help each other.

Precautions and Possible Pitfalls

 It is always difficult to define who "slow learners" are, and if or when teachers do, these students may be stigmatized by other teachers and/or their peers. So reading teachers must be careful not to tell these students that they are "slow" and treat them as usual learners that have a different reading curriculum. In addition, Kathleen and Robert Cooter (2004, p. 683) caution teachers to be mindful that slower learners can "master reading skills only after massed and distributed practice over time." Thus, teachers must be patient with their students' progress.

Source

Cooter, K. S., & Cooter, R. B. (2004). One size doesn't fit all: Slow learners in the reading classroom. *The Reading Teacher, 57*(7), 680–684.

Strategy 33: Create a partnership between general education teachers and special educators using a shared classroom literacy program.

What the Research Says

 Roberta Schnorr and Linda Davern (2005) suggest that exemplary literacy classrooms should have the following features: a respectful and supportive community, appropriate levels of challenge and support, use of multiple methods and materials, and expert instruction in processes as well as reading skills. They further maintain that developing such classroom environments with 20 to 30 students is best accomplished by having two professionals working in a productive partnership as opposed to one working in isolation. Schnorr and Davern (2005) have observed many positive effects when the classroom teacher teams in a systematic and thoughtful way with another professional, such as a special educator or literacy specialist.

Classroom Applications

Schnorr and Davern (2005) point out that successful teams operate from a shared knowledge of effective practices, and a shared understanding of the fundamentals of teaming. They say that the first step in collaborative planning is to explore recommended literacy practices for all the classroom learners, including so-called struggling readers. For Schnorr and Davern (2005, p. 495), effective literacy practices include the following:

> *Classroom context matters:* valued membership in a respectful, caring community supports student learning and motivation.

> *Effective literacy programs are comprehensive:* all students benefit from an instructional framework.

> *Students who have difficulty learning to read do not usually require different kinds of instruction:* more often, they need application of the same principles by someone who can apply them expertly to individual children.

They further suggest that it is important to discuss the importance of valued membership for each child, drawing on students' strengths, and providing tasks that are challenging.

Precautions and Possible Pitfalls

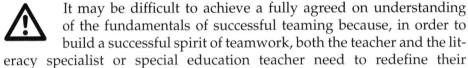 It may be difficult to achieve a fully agreed on understanding of the fundamentals of successful teaming because, in order to build a successful spirit of teamwork, both the teacher and the literacy specialist or special education teacher need to redefine their roles and responsibilities, and this may take a lot of time to negotiate. In addition, it is not entirely clear why supplemental services for struggling readers is not provided or how these struggling readers are helped in the common instruction.

Source

Schnorr, R., & Davern, L. (2005). Creating exemplary literacy classrooms through the power of teaming. *The Reading Teacher, 58,* 494–506.

7

Help for English-Language Learners

No matter how busy you may think you are, you must find time for reading, or surrender yourself to self-chosen ignorance.

—Atwood H. Townsend

 Strategy 34: Explore the definition of literacy and the complexity of the term when applied to bilingual and bicultural students.

What the Research Says

Jimenez (2003) argues for a broader look at how we interpret and define the term literacy. He states that the more formalized statements of literacy aren't "disinterested and detached musings" but rather active rhetorical efforts to legitimize the status quo and continue the privileges enjoyed by specific groups. His argument hints at a veiled form of institutional racism. Jimenez traces the interests of those who define literacy back to their identities, which draw from, reflect, or are shaped by their ethnicity, race, class, gender, or other factors. He believes that current definitions of literacy do nothing to advance the academic achievement of marginalized groups; rather, these mainstream definitions serve only to continue current institutionalized inequities. Jimenez's work is an anecdotal and literature-based exploration of attitudes toward literacy as they relate to bilingual and bicultural populations, specifically Latinos.

Jimenez identified some student groups as contributing to their own failure with an attitude that appropriate school-based forms of literacy need to be resisted as a form of domestication. Many other individuals have been defined socially and economically on the basis of their failure to acquire standard forms of English, Spanish, and other necessary levels of literacy, or, increasingly today, knowledge of technologies.

Many individuals and groups, Jimenez claims, have equally sophisticated but unrecognized abilities that should be incorporated into an updated definition of literacy. He supports the idea that literacy researchers can contribute to the literacy discussion by identifying the unrecognized abilities students from diverse backgrounds bring to schools.

In support of Jimenez's view, Bean (2001) points to "The sharply demarcated distance between students' multiple literacy's outside of school and the sanctioned text-based, canonical literacy's inside the walls creates an artificial education where students 'do school' to succeed" (p. 7).

Classroom Applications

In today's educational environment of high-stakes testing, teachers have less and less choice in what and sometimes how they teach. While Jimenez brings up some really good points, the reality of today's classrooms often means teaching a narrow band of mandated content, experiences, and related skills. Expanding the range of skills and knowledge that define literacy would seem to fly against today's political grain. However, individual teachers can begin to acknowledge and even celebrate diverse backgrounds, especially their students' own unique literacy-based and communication-based cultural experiences. Acknowledging, highlighting, legitimizing, and expanding the range of multiple literacies and competencies within diverse populations can expand the range of options teachers have for supporting school-based literacy.

Research cited and described by Jimenez defined "out-of-school" literacies as a treasure trove of experiences and information with benefits for students and teachers. Out-of-school literacies exhibited by mainstream students are well known to teachers, and teachers can take advantage of these skills to promote school-based literacy. Mainstream students and teachers often see the same films, watch the same television shows, and generally share many cultural experiences that narrowly define literacy.

Some examples of out-of-school literacy skills illustrate a wider definition of literacy that teachers can build on. Often bilingual and bicultural students are depended on by their families for negotiating the demands of the English language and other cultural literacies. They often serve as translators for rental and lease agreements, income tax forms, and many other commercial transactions. They also aid in oral translations in stressful or fast-paced interactions. All these functions can be seen as alternative literacies. Many bilingual and bicultural students take these types of literacy seriously and see themselves as important contributors to the family.

These out-of-school literacies can serve to build bridges to improve literacy instruction. Questions remain about the relationship between these practices and literacy practices commonly found in schools, centering on how this knowledge can be worked into curriculum or if it even should be.

Precautions and Possible Pitfalls

 Very little guidance and few rules exist for the teacher who wants to explore these concepts. In many states, literacy issues are hotly debated. Teachers need to be able to understand their local schools' or departments' political climates to know what they can do and what they can't. Every school is different in its curricular view and how it values diverse identities.

Sources

Bean, T. W. (2001). An update on reading in the content areas: Social constructionist dimensions. *Reading Online, 5*(5). Accessed February 28, 2006 at: http://www.readingonline.org/

Jimenez, R. T. (2003). Literacy and the Latino students in the United States: Some considerations, questions, and new directions. *Reading Research Quarterly, 38,* 122–130.

Strategy 35: In multicultural classrooms, reflect on the literacy instructional practices of the countries your students come from and how these practices affect their performance in U.S. schools.

What the Research Says

The research of Smith and coworkers (2003) points to a lack of attention paid to language and literacy practices ethnic and linguistic-minority students bring from their countries of origin. These practices are often considered barriers to the types of literacy valued in U.S. schools. The authors explained that recent studies have discovered benefits for incorporating linguistic and other aspects of nonmainstream cultures into instruction. In their research they further examined the idea that educators can explore their own understanding of reading and writing, and how to teach these subjects, by considering the practices of other countries. They selected Mexico for their work because it is the country of origin for many Hispanic students and families.

The authors stated that as Spanish-speaking children continue to increase in number, it is important to find out what they have been taught. In their study, they conducted a qualitative literacy practice (writing, speaking, and reading) study in a small city in central Mexico. Over a period of six months, they collected data within first- and fourth-grade classrooms in two neighboring schools with different socioeconomic populations. The first school had students from working-class parents generally considered of indigenous heritage. The second school was a private Montessori school attended by children of middle-class and professional parents. Classroom observations and interviews served as data collection. Finally, to better understand how the school-based literacy practices observed fit into the culture, researchers studied the surrounding community, comparing school and locally produced texts (signs, advertising, banners, etc.). In this way the researchers could contrast and compare different uses of oral and written language within the modalities of reading, writing, and speaking. The following is a summary of the study's findings.

Writing was generally highly controlled in both schools, and writing centered on short, discrete texts, typically dictation or copying of teacher-produced models. Students were rarely allowed to write texts longer than a sentence. They saw no examples of student writing for communicative purposes or the "authoring" function of writing. The greatest concern was the correctness of form, spelling, punctuation, and accent marks.

In contrast to the writing, spoken language was used as the medium of choice for expressive communication. There were few limitations on what students were allowed to say or how they said it.

Reading was not as controlled as the students' writing or as free as spoken language at either school. However, there was no "free-reading" or sustained silent reading like you might find in the United States. Free reading was always a solitary activity reserved for the end of lessons. Children were never asked to comment on or write about something they read. Oral reading was treated like written language and it was highly monitored. Errors in pronunciation were corrected and, somewhat as in writing, form (a public display of literacy) was more important than comprehension and content. The authors also mentioned that excessive reading for extended periods could be seen as antisocial behavior.

Written text in the community was seen and treated very differently from how literacy is viewed in schools. It was treated more like spoken language in schools, largely unmonitored for form, structure, and content. Parents also expressed more concern for form, spelling, handwriting, and so on than for content or expression. "Correctness" was a bigger concern than meaning for most parents. Overall, the parent's view of reading seemed to match a self-critical belief that Mexico is not a country of readers. These views were reflected across the socioeconomic strata of the study in both schools.

Classroom Applications

Knowing what the study has learned about reading and writing in Mexico, teachers should understand that multicultural students and their families might have a different notion of writing and reading from native English speakers. We need to remember and keep in mind that many parents new to U.S. schools are literate in their first language, and that literacy and education have been prized and valued in their culture. However, many of these parents (and some of their older children) experienced literacy education in ways we think of as provincial, quaint, and even ineffective and boring. Knowing this can help explain observations teachers may not understand.

Teachers who take advantage of this cultural knowledge can create opportunities for transnational students to transition into U.S. classrooms and literacy instruction in a kinder, more gentle and understanding way. Teachers can take the opportunity to talk to students about the different literacy practices in the two countries. Teachers and students can actually explore literacy practices to locate differences. This includes listening to students' reactions to classroom instruction and language as it is used in their communities of origin.

It might be interesting for teachers to analyze academic texts produced for use in other countries. While an invasion of Spanish translations of English books, textbooks, and other teaching materials is occurring in Mexico and other Hispanic countries, very little comes to the United States from these countries. The trend is sometimes referred to as the "Disney-fication" of children's literature in Latin America (Dorfman & Mattelart, 1991). It is also probably true that literacy and literacy instruction vary from country to county.

Providing accommodations for linguistic and literate diversity does not need to be a serious challenge for classroom teachers. If anything, it can create a clear understanding of performance trends a teacher might observe among students in their classrooms. Teachers can see this knowledge as an opportunity to reexamine performances of their students and their instructional strategies.

Precautions and Possible Pitfalls

Teaching a range of literacies is messy for a content teacher. Just teaching a student to read a textbook is clear and straightforward. Expository textbook writing is usually consistent and predictable from one chapter to the next. Multiple literacy means that on one day you will be teaching listening skills and note taking, and on another you will be teaching students how to gauge the validity of a website and its text as well as intellectual property rights and plagiarism.

In the real world, no one single approach works with all children. However, teachers working collaboratively as a group, with parents of their students, can begin to understand and address the literacy needs of their communities. Teachers need to respect and support parents' efforts to educate their children at home even though it may not match what is happening at school.

Sources

Anderson, J., & Gunderson, L. (2001). "You don't read a science book, you study it": Exploring cultural concepts of reading. *Reading Online, 4*(7). Accessed at: http://www.readingonline.org/

Dorfman, A., & Mattelart, A.(1991). *How to read Donald Duck: Imperialist ideology in the Disney comic.* New York: International General; originally published in 1971 as *Para Leer al Pato Donald.* Valparaiso, Chile: Ediciones Universitarias de Valparíso.

Smith, P. H., Jiménez, R. T., & Martínez-León, N. (2003). Other countries' literacies: What U.S. educators can learn from Mexican schools. *The Reading Teacher, 56*(8), 772–781.

Strategy 36: Consider the variety of elements that support literacy intervention for young English-language learners.

What the Research Says

The purpose of the Alanis (2003) study was to help explain the effectiveness of a highly focused early intervention for first-grade ELLs with reading difficulties. The goal was to identify the essential components supporting the student's gains in performance outcomes. The research represented two distinct efforts along the Texas-Mexico border. One school used university-based tutors and the second school relied on the expertise of the classroom teacher. The overall driving questions were, What are the effects of supplemental reading instruction for first-grade Spanish-speaking readers in bilingual programs? and What are the critical instructional components for developing reading skills in ELLs?

Participants in one school included five preservice teachers enrolled in an instructional methods college course that served 25 first-grade Spanish speaking students. During the course of the research, two tutors dropped from the program and the remaining three tutors worked with 13 of the 25 students.

In the second school, a fully certified bilingual classroom teacher with 20 years' experience also worked with 13 students.

Classroom Applications

Alanis (2003) stated the results of study demonstrated that it is possible to facilitate literacy development in struggling first graders in a relatively short period of time. Alanis (2003) also listed the components of a reading intervention that were crucial to any intervention program:

- The intervention is frequent and of a sufficient time to make a difference.
- Student-to-teacher (tutor) ratio is small (1 to 4).
- Texts are carefully selected and sequenced to ensure student success.
- Word learning or vocabulary activities are used to help children become familiar with print.
- Writing is used to teach and extend word identification skills.

- Assessment is meaningful, practical, and ongoing.
- Students build confidence and see themselves as readers.
- Culturally responsive principles of instruction must be embedded in the model.
- Use of the "mother tongue" must be incorporated into the reading intervention in the case of ELLs.

Source

Alanis, I. (Winter 2003). Preventing reading failure for English language learners: Interventions for struggling first-grade L2 students. *NABE Journal of Research,* 92–109.

Strategy 37: Don't forget visual texts or "reading pictures," either literary or factual, can be a powerful medium for learning and can assist L2 learners' literacy development.

What the Research Says

Walsh's (2003) small study examined the oral responses of young children to the texts of two narrative picture books, *I Went Walking* (Machin, 1989) and *Felix and Alexander* (Denton, 1985). Walsh (2003) cited a single question that guided her research, "What does the 'reading' of pictures reveal compared with the reading of print?" Her findings emphasize how images can evolve different levels of response. The data for this study was taken from a larger study (Walsh, 1997) conducted in several primary schools in Sydney, Australia. The 2003 study featured the responses of children from kindergarten and first grade, while the larger study investigated the beginning reading behavior of young second-language learners compared to native English speakers. A theoretical framework of reader-related variables was compared to reading behavior, both qualitatively and quantitatively. A framework of text-related variables for narrative picture books was proposed and compared with oral responses to these books, and some of these students' oral responses were examined for the Walsh paper, to determine which responses appeared to be specific to the verbal or visual features of the text.

Walsh's findings emphasize how images can evoke a variety of levels of response. According to Walsh, the study confirms that teachers need to reconsider the nature of reading and reading education in an environment where words and print are no longer the dominant medium of knowledge transfer. Images take on a much bigger role in the transfer of information.

It should also be noted that many of the children in this study were L2 learners. The L2 learners responded with the same range of comments and understandings as the L1 students. They did not, however, have the same mastery of language structures as L1 students. They were able to infer and evaluate and develop the conceptual process of reading. Therefore, the research found picture books offered a rich resource to assist L2 students in their understanding of "content" knowledge, cultural practices, and linguistic structures of English.

Classroom Applications

While this study deals with very young readers and a small educational scope, it is interesting to consider a wider and important context for this small study. Based on the idea that visual images and multimedia are a language, visual literacy can be defined as the ability to understand and produce visual messages. This skill is becoming increasingly important with the ever-proliferating mass media in society. As more and more information and entertainment is acquired through nonprint media (such as television, movies, and the Internet), the ability to think critically and visually about the images presented becomes a crucial skill. Based on this small study, visual literacy is something that can be taught and learned, just as reading and writing are learned. Although not taught in schools (yet), the ability to process visual images efficiently and understand the impact they have on viewers are nevertheless very important.

From the beginnings of human culture, visual awareness has been a key element in communication. Just as information conveyed by the written word held significance for humanity in the twentieth century, the symbols of early cave paintings held a deep significance for the artists and cultures that produced them. Over time, these symbols and meanings evolved into the alphabets of today; which are the basis for verbal literacy.

To be verbally literate, one must be able to manipulate the basic components of written language: the letters, words, spelling, grammar, syntax. With mastery of these elements of written communication, the possibilities of verbal expression are endless. Visual literacy in the twenty-first century operates within the same boundaries. Just as verbal literacy depends on basic components and common meanings, visual literacy involves basic elements and common meaning.

Twenty-first-century literacies refer to the skills needed to flourish in today's society and in the future. Discrete yet integrated literacy disciplines have emerged around information, media, multicultural paradigms, and specific professional workplaces, all of which require a specialized and often unique visual literacy. This range requires the combination of these literacies to help K–12 students and adult learners address the issues and solve the problems that confront them.

As a "language," visual literacy can be defined as the ability to understand and produce visual messages. This skill is becoming increasingly important with the proliferation of mass media in society. As we acquire more and more information and entertainment through nonprint media (such as television, movies, and the Internet), the ability to think critically and visually about the images presented becomes a significant skill. It is very important to be able to process visual images efficiently and understand their impact on viewers. The suggestions in this section provide teachers with a starting point in the learning process.

Rather than simply transcribing print from page to screen, students will work with still and moving images, graphics, and text. Organizing and arranging these elements on the screen requires expertise in visual language and human perception. It requires individuals who are skilled in the design and display of electronically produced, stored, and accessed information.

In an age when most Americans get most of their information from television not textbooks, pictures not print, we need a wider definition of what it means to be literate. Many of us grew up with such adages as *you can't judge a book by its cover* and *a picture is worth a thousand words.* These words are even truer today in an age of not only computers and telecommunications but virtual reality and "imageneering." Today's technologies represent a startling fusion of sight and sound that frequently makes it difficult for us to discern illusion from reality, fact from fiction. Special effects in movies such as *JFK* and *Forrest Gump* merge the past with the present, color with black and white, the dead with the living, and fact with fiction in such a way that the real truth can often be confused with the "reel truth."

While such techniques may render the program more visually pleasing, they represent the emergence of infotainment and the decline of objective, neutral, and reliable news. Given these trends, responsible citizens need to possess the ability to question the accuracy and authenticity of information in all its forms, not just print. They need the ability to make reflective critical responses to this information. But media literacy is about more than just consuming information. A media-literate individual is able to produce, create, and successfully communicate information in all its forms, not just print. The emergence of CD-ROM technology is a simple example of why these skills are now necessary. This technology fuses two previously discrete technologies, the computer and the video camera, as well as two information formats, print and picture.

Media literacy promotes the critical thinking skills necessary to understand the complex issues facing modern society. Frequently the media oversimplified these complexities. *U.S. News and World Report,* for example, has said that "Television is so focused on pictures and so limited by them, that in a normal run of reporting it cannot begin to provide the context that gives meaning and perspective."

The old adage "the camera never lies" is indicative of how we have been conditioned to accept the relationship between reality and its representations in the media. In a day of virtual reality and computer simulations, seeing is *not* believing. All media are carefully assembled, edited, selected, and designed constructions. They show us a world that is a selected and often unrepresentative view even though it seems to be true. Learning to distinguish the reality from its reflection is essential.

Leading educator Theodore Sizer has noted that "television has become the biggest school system, the principal shaper of culture . . . powerfully influencing the young on what it is to be American. Understanding what television and other media teach is central to this component of media literacy."

While no specific "classroom applications" are suggested here, it is wise to begin to consider how you can think about visual literacy and how your curriculum might reflect a shift toward integrating elements of visual literacy education. The following websites offer additional discourse and links to those thinking about visual literacy topics:

Center for Media Literacy. Retrieved April 11, 2003, from http://www.medialit.org

21st Century Schools. Accessed February 15, 2006 at: http://www.21stcenturyschools.com/ (a list of visual literacy links)

Tasmania Department of Education. Accessed February 15, 2006 at: http://www.education.tas.gov.au/ (ideas for seven- and eight-year-olds in English)

Precautions and Possible Pitfalls

 Literacy is seen by most as the ability to read and write. The definition is changing to include the new ways film, television, and the Internet communicate ideas and information. Literacy is painted with a wider brush in the twenty-first century. Parents may need to be enlightened to this newer and wider literacy paradigm. Take the time to educate them along with your students.

Source

Walsh, M. (2003). "Reading" pictures: what do they reveal? Young children's reading of visual texts. *Literacy, 37*(1), 123–134.

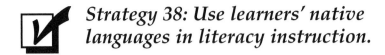

Strategy 38: Use learners' native languages in literacy instruction.

What the Research Says

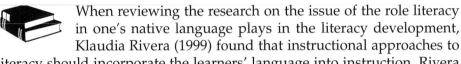

When reviewing the research on the issue of the role literacy in one's native language plays in the literacy development, Klaudia Rivera (1999) found that instructional approaches to literacy should incorporate the learners' language into instruction. Rivera suggests that learners may benefit from their native language literacy skills because they can transfer basic skills, in reading for example, from their first to their second language. She further suggests that literacy teachers should, in fact, promote biliteracy in their classes.

Classroom Applications

Teachers who use the learners' native language as a positive influence on literacy acquisition must place their native language and cultural background and experiences at the center of the program. Teachers can achieve this by involving the students in generating materials for use in class, having them connect the literacy activities to their oral language, culture, and prior experiences. The teacher could develop a theme, such as health or immigration, for the literacy curriculum and ask the learners to contribute to the theme by developing and producing a video documenting their views, experiences, and research on that theme. Teachers can use the learners' native language in beginning-level language classes as a means of helping students with basic vocabulary related to the project's theme. In this way, literacy in their native language and ESL are taught together, usually by a bilingual teacher. There are other ways that young literacy learners can be instructed, such as keeping the learners in their native language literacy classes until they reach a proficient level of reading and then transferring them to ESL classes. This second method emphasizes literacy development first in the child's native language, which in turn can help literacy acquisition in English (Rivera, 1999).

Precautions and Possible Pitfalls

Because the learners' native language is used at the beginning literacy levels, the classes may need to be team taught with a bilingual teacher, so it is important to coordinate such lessons carefully by planning ahead and even practicing together before the lesson takes place. Depending on their level of English literacy proficiency, learners may need to stay in their native literacy classes until they have reached sufficient proficiency in reading and writing in English. Teachers must also be aware of what they are trying to achieve by using the learners' native language as a source of instruction: to develop literacy in both languages or literacy only in English.

Source

Rivera, K. (1999). From developing one's voice to making oneself heard: Affecting language policy from the bottom up. In T. Huebner & K. Davis (Eds.), *Sociopolitical perspectives on language policy and language planning in the USA* (pp. 333–346). Amsterdam: Benjamins.

 Strategy 39: For second-language learners, teach reading before testing it.

What the Research Says

 Urquhart and Weir (2002) point out that a typical reading lesson in many classrooms can consist of the teacher presenting the students with a reading text with no real previous discussion. The students subsequently read the text, and the the teacher asks questions, usually comprehension type questions, and the feedback students get is usually limited to being told if their answers were correct or not; in fact, this is informal assessment rather than teaching of reading. We feel this lesson sequence is somewhat misguided; teaching should come *before* assessment, with exploration of, among other aspects of reading, various strategies to arrive at a desired correct answer.

Classroom Applications

Studies reported by Urquhart and Weir (2002) suggest that reading strategies can be taught to students, and when taught, these reading strategies can help improve student performance on the tests of comprehension and recall that can only follow the teaching. Winograd and Hare (1988) have called for second-language teachers to explain to the students the following:

What the strategy is. This involves description of the strategy.

Why a strategy should be learned. Students should be reminded frequently about the benefits of using the strategy. If we teach strategies without direct explanation and explicit teacher modeling for a short period, it would not have a long-term effect on students' strategy use and would thus not help them develop as strategic readers.

How to effectively use the strategy. One method is for the teacher to model the strategy in a thinking-aloud manner. For this, the teacher would tell the class exactly what he or she is doing in using the strategy.

When and *where* a strategy should be used.

How to evaluate successful (or unsuccessful) use of the strategy.

Precautions and Possible Pitfalls

 Teachers of second-language reading strategies must be very careful to reinforce the strategies that they teach; otherwise they will have no long-term effect on students. It is no use to explain a strategy one time, then to go on to another strategy, and so on. It is vital that teachers continually reinforce strategies covered in class so that their students can use them independently and when called for in tests.

Sources

Urquhart, A. H., and Weir, C. J. (2002). *Reading in a second language: Process, product and practice*. New York: Longman.

Winograd, P., & Hare, V. (1988). Direct instruction of reading comprehension strategies: The nature of teacher explanation. In C. E. Weinstein, E. T. Goetz, & P. A. Alexander (Eds.), *Learning and study strategies: Issues in assessment instruction and evaluation* (pp. 121–139). San Diego: Academic Press.

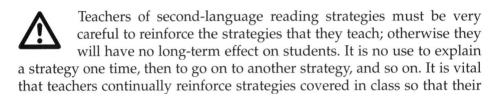 *Strategy 40: Use similarities between Spanish and English to facilitate spelling instruction.*

What the Research Says

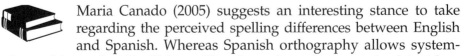 Maria Canado (2005) suggests an interesting stance to take regarding the perceived spelling differences between English and Spanish. Whereas Spanish orthography allows systematic teaching rules, English spelling is perhaps best acquired incidentally, through exposure in extensive voluntary reading. She notes that the Spanish orthographic system is more transparent, presenting a much more notable phoneme-grapheme correspondence than English, while the

English orthographic system lacks orthographic regularity—spelling does not mirror the pronunciation of words, therefore, additional knowledge of specific lexical items is required, along with some understanding of morphemic structure.

However, in what she calls the "dual-route or dual-process framework," she points out striking similarities between English and Spanish spelling. She suggests that two separate processing systems can be employed to spell, and these pathways operate in parallel and are linked but can be dissociated:

> The phonological module or route deals with spelling of consistent or regular words and for the production of unfamiliar words.

> The visual-orthographic strategy or procedure involves words whose spellings have been memorized and is responsible for generating familiar words that are retrieved from the memory store as single units.

For a speller to be successful in both English and Spanish, he or she must master both phonological and visual modules. Canado (2005) maintains that incorrect operation of either of these processes might explain misspelling in either English or Spanish.

Classroom Applications

 Canado (2005) says that spelling should be considered not as an isolated subject but integrated with the broader language arts curriculum. Teachers should use different genres that present diverse words and combine visual, auditory, and tactile or kinesthetic activities in teaching methods, to address both routes to acquiring orthography: the phonological (e.g., through "tick what you hear" exercises) and visual or lexical one (by means of word searches, for instance).

Precautions and Possible Pitfalls

Canado (2005) recognizes that it may be difficult to keep a high enough level of difficulty of words for children to misspell that will also provide better insight on the logic they are using to spell. She further suggests that lots of repetition of the rules and strategies is essential to achieve spelling success.

Source

Canado, M. (2005). English and Spanish spelling: Are they really different? *The Reading Teacher, 58,* 522–530.

8

Literacy Instruction and Assessment Across the Curriculum

The man who does not read good books has no advantage over the man who can't read them.

—Mark Twain

 Strategy 41: When grading a student's writing, consider what the student is able to do well before noting what needs improvement.

What the Research Says

In a review of current research, Gregg and Mather (2002) noted that many factors influence the perception that a student is not a proficient writer. They propose that, by considering writing skills (spelling, syntax, vocabulary, etc.) as well as the task format (dictating, copying, timed writing, etc.), teachers will discover a student's writing strengths and also notice areas that require support. They

note that it is vital to remember that writing is integrally related to social interactions and dialogue. In other words, writing is not simply the attempt to represent linguistic structures such as sentences, words, or phonemes; written expression requires a social process achieved through dialogue and interaction.

Classroom Applications

Students with disabilities often view writing as a hated task, and as standards move toward embedding writing in more curricular areas, poor writing skills can lead to a broader dislike of school and classwork in general. Writing itself is a very personal enterprise, and for a student who struggles with it, writing can be a very personal failure.

When teaching writing, teachers should pay close attention to how students view themselves as writers and encourage them to focus on finding and writing in their own unique voice. By modeling the writing process for them—showing how ideas come first, then a rough draft to give the ideas shape, followed by an editing process that addresses the mechanical aspects of the writing—teachers can begin to facilitate student success.

When assessing written assignments, teachers should consider grading the first draft for content only, engaging the student in a written dialogue about what the student is saying in his or her writing. Teachers must quell their urges to point out paragraphing, capitalization, and spelling errors as they read. They should demonstrate the difference between content and mechanics by isolating them in the teaching and assessment/evaluation process.

Experienced teachers recognize that writing skill develops on a continuum, and they help their students to see individual growth along that continuum. Students who understand that what they have to say is unique and valuable are much more likely to risk committing their thoughts and ideas to paper. They know that the mechanical components of writing can be addressed concretely farther along in their writing process.

Precautions and Possible Pitfalls

In recent years, many teachers and parents have lamented the lack of spelling and grammar instruction in schools. Students need to learn the principles behind spelling patterns as well as the basic grammatical components of standard written English. Most students learn these basic rules more effectively in context, so teachers should consider embedding a lesson on a specific rule of grammar by asking the students to correct it or apply it in their own writing.

Source

Gregg, N., & Mather, N. (2002). School is fun at recess. *Journal of Learning Disabilities,* 35(1), 7–23.

Strategy 42: Consider the use of open-book tests to promote and encourage the assigned textbook reading and the skills required to quickly find and utilize information.

What the Research Says

 This study involved 1080 community college students enrolled in general biology classes over a 10-year period. Gregory Phillips (2006) was interested in finding out if three open-book tests over the length of the course could be used to improve study skills and if the students with weaker study skills benefited more than students with moderate or stronger study skills. The mean improvement for the entire sample was 4.47 points; the students with weak study skills improved an average of 23.79 points, the students with moderate study skills improved 4.88 points, and the students designated as strong decreased 4.88 points. The most obvious reason for the improvement with the weak and moderate group stems from their being provided with study strategies and an opportunity to turn those strategies into skills. The most dramatic improvement was seen between the first and second open-book test of the year. Phillips assumed that students with strong study skills were not assimilating any new strategies or they were not incorporating any new skills. However, after a drop in scores in the second test they rebounded for the third test. Although they did not show an improvement in their overall study skills, their drop was minimal.

Classroom Applications

Phillips (2006) used his open-book tests as a vehicle for teaching study skills within only the three tests that made up a portion of overall class evaluation. These open-book tests targeted information that was related to lectures but not directly covered during class. Also, he prepared students by going over examples of open-book questions and discussing strategies for effectively and efficiently using the class text. Finally, Phillips made the importance of completing the assigned readings clear early in the class.

He also taught instruction strategies for comprehending the layout of the targeted chapters and highlighting, tabbing, using the index as well as the significance of bolded pages and bolded keywords within the text. The open-book test questions also contained contextual clues that directed the students to the correct chapters and subheadings. Students who used the study skills and read the material prior to the test could more quickly narrow their search.

You can see that Phillips's efforts were not typical of college and university classrooms. In this class instruction, goals included not only teaching the subject matter but also providing students with the study skills necessary to help them learn. To do this, teachers need to see testing, assessment, and evaluation as an opportunity to embed teaching and learning devices within the targeted learning processes. This may take a change in perspective regarding using tests for evaluation purposes only. The rewards students take with them can be seen as greater than just subject matter knowledge.

A variation of this technique, is to give students test essay questions a few days before the test. Use those questions as an opportunity to teach study strategies. In this example, consider giving them 10 essay questions out of which only two or three will be used on the actual test. They won't know which ones they will see come test day.

There are many other ways to incorporate the literacy-specific study skill agenda into testing. Again, you just need to see testing in a new way beyond mere assessment.

Precautions and Possible Pitfalls

 Sometimes more successful students, especially in secondary schools, feel their study skills work just fine and are not open to new or different ideas. If you try to push your agenda too hard, you will lose them and they will lose respect for the rigor of the class. You'll have to decide on the needs of the class, do your best to help those in need, and move on. Better test scores should reinforce and reward those who assimilate more effective study skills.

Source

Phillips, G. (2006). Using open-book tests to strengthen the study skills of community college biology students. *Journal of Adolescent & Adult Literacy, 49*(7), 574–582.

Strategy 43: Move beyond the simplistic notion of a "balanced approach to literacy instruction" and explore more fully what it means to be a literate person and how we can help students.

What the Research Says

Rasinski and Padak (2004) state that scholars appear to have reached consensus that a balanced approach to reading instruction reflects the greatest promise for improving literacy instruction. In their view, the "balanced approach" includes instructional components in phonics or word decoding, fluency, and comprehension. While they agree with the approach, they feel the issue of balance in literacy is much more complex than current instructional models and literature may suggest. They argue that a more comprehensive consideration of literacy instruction is needed. To be comprehensive, literacy needs to be integrated within the literacy curriculum itself. It must be integrated into all facets of the classroom and school's learning environment. Further, literacy instruction needs to be integrated with both the home and community environment. The authors state that literacy instruction is more than just balancing classroom strategies; balance and comprehensiveness go hand in hand in all aspects of the students' lives.

Classroom Applications

Balanced literacy curriculum and instruction are, by consensus, very hot topics in literacy education. *Balanced reading instruction* has many meanings, and many versions of such programs exist. To many teachers, the term describes attempts to establish equity between literacy instruction mechanics (such as phonics, spelling, and comprehension strategies) and the more holistic strategies involving process writing, literature-based instruction, and reader reflection for meaning. To others, including the media, it means teaching that combines phonics instruction, phonemic awareness strategies, and spelling. Fitzgerald (1999) defines balanced reading instruction as a philosophical perspective that includes three wide categories of beliefs:

- that children should possess certain global abilities, such as understanding and responding to what they read;
- that children should have certain local abilities, such as word identification routines and strategies; and
- that children should have a love of reading or a knowledge of reading.

As appealing as the balanced approach to literacy may be after years of discussions about reading instruction, we need to remember that the concept of balance is considerably more complex than it appears at first glance, especially for the classroom teacher. The balanced approach concept may be simple and appear obvious, giving students everything that has been demonstrated to work, but in reality it involves much more than disparate approaches to instruction. While dedicating 30 minutes to word decoding and phonics balanced against equal time devoted to guided reading may be appealing, this approach may not produce the desired results. In sixth grade, for example, giving more attention to guided reading and less to phonics and decoding, yet teaching both, may be more beneficial. In middle school, it might be more appropriate to spend time negotiating meaning and comprehension. In high school, contrasting and comparing similar readings in a reflection paper may be appropriate for measuring comprehension.

It's clear that the truth is in the details when considering what the real meaning of "balanced" is. Beyond the surface of consensus on balanced reading curriculum is a huge range of options that teachers need to consider. Maybe the term *comprehensive literacy curriculum* better describes the complex and interrelated nature of the types of literacy philosophy we should strive for within a "balanced" approach. Consider how a balanced philosophy, as a working strategy, could be applied within the following important instructional considerations.

School/Community/Home:
Balanced Literacy Throughout the Day and the Year

Most examples of balanced curriculum consider literacy only within the boundaries of the classroom, school, and school year. We all know students spend the largest part of their day and year outside of the classroom. In a comprehensive program, educators need to take into account the home and support the parents and the community give year-round in helping students learn to read and write.

It's no secret that parents are most involved with their children in their early years, the preschool years before formal school begins and during the elementary school years. If we want parents involved in secondary schools, we need to develop a pattern of involvement and target parents during these timeframes. Learning to read before school begins requires parent involvement. Preschool children develop basic literacy concepts and conventions and especially phonemic relationships before formal school begins. Common sense tells us that this gives children an advantage once school begins.

The exact role parents and community play can vary, however, the obvious example is parents reading to their children. This is just the beginning in developing a home-school component. The home needs to support literacy instruction at school and school needs to support literacy instruction at home. Teachers need to recommend activities that tie into school content, literacy skills, and strategies that are part of the school instruction. Again, Rasinski and Padak (2004) found that parents appreciate specific and concrete suggestions from teachers. For example, parents can work with local libraries to help students get library cards. Teachers need to be fairly specific and direct in communicating advice for the home environment. This is especially true over the long periods of time during holidays and summer. Literacy activities can be practiced at home and teachers can encourage parents to model reading and writing behaviors as well as sending literacy tips home. These might include book list suggestions. The bottom line is to help parents and students connect what goes on in school and what goes on in the community and home.

Balanced Instruction Within Instructional Cooperative Learning Groups

What does balance within cooperative grouping practices look like? Most would agree that one-on-one or small-group strategies offer teachers the most direct means of targeting instruction at the specific needs of students. However, is it a good idea to keep struggling learners grouped together for a long time? Won't these students begin to feel a sense of failure or lack of self-esteem by being segregated from the more advanced students? Also, when students are not the focus of the teacher's attention, they might not be fully engaged in productive reading activity.

How does whole-group instruction work? Most teachers aim instructional strategies toward the middle of the academic range. Students at either end of the achievement spectrum receive work that is either too easy or very frustrating. Some students are also presented with content they are not ready to learn and some already know the content. Also, quiet students in large classes often are ignored and teachers sometimes assume they understand the lesson while their understanding may be only superficial.

Most would agree that, in general, cooperative small-group instruction provides the students with the greatest opportunity for achievement. A balanced literacy approach would seem to dictate a call for small-group instruction with the smallest teacher-student ratio possible. During other times of the day, maybe in other content areas, teachers can have students work individually, in pairs, in heterogeneous small groups, and in whole groups. Balance can be achieved and the variety of teacher and student contacts can be maximized.

Balanced Instruction in Reading Genre and Text Types

What does a balanced approach to choice of reading genres or texts types look like? In most school settings, narrative fiction, or stories, tend to be the norm. Literacy practices today call for expanding the range of what is considered reading or literacy activities. The variety of other text genres that students can read and use as a model for writing is huge and getting bigger. Magazines, scripts, newspapers, picture books, electronic texts, and multimedia all can be sources of curriculum. At the far end of the spectrum, you can include charts, tables, graphs, signs, and maps. Most would agree that in a balanced program, nonfiction, informational texts, and poetry should be included along with narrative fiction. Is this too restrictive? The big questions to ask are what texts should be used in reading instruction and why. What does balanced and comprehensive look like?

The Affective Domain

Beyond just setting up learning environments to teach students to read and write lies the greater goal of helping students become lifelong readers and writers. This goal suggests a definite affective component to literacy instruction. Nurturing life-long reading and writing potential in students involves more than just mastering a set of skills within your curriculum and assessment. We know students who like to read and write will read and write more and will develop fluency and intellectual growth as a result of increased literacy.

So in addition to helping students master skills, a truly balanced approach must develop students' desire to read and write and a love of the written word that continues well beyond the classroom. Sometimes this component is missing from school literacy programs. Find time to model your own positive reading experiences and facilitate reading and writing in ways that enable students to see they are learning skills to create a richer and more satisfying life for themselves.

Balanced Instruction for Wide Range of Learners in the Same Classroom

All teachers, at all grade levels, know that students are not equal in the literacy skills they bring to the instructional environment. A truly equitable program requires a differentiated approach, and a critical element of such an approach is time. Students who struggle need more time than those students who have fewer difficulties. Struggling readers read fewer words than students who do not experience difficulty. If they are not given more help and time, they will never catch up with the more advanced readers. Equal time on task for all does not mean fairness. Check out various models of reading recovery programs and you will find examples of how creative educators try to accommodate struggling readers.

Balanced Literacy Instruction in the Content Areas Across the School Day

In many instructional settings, reading time significantly outweighs writing instruction time. In a truly balanced and comprehensive approach, reading and writing should carry equal weight. In addition, in secondary school content areas, reading and writing should be balanced within content delivery. Teachers are often so concerned with "covering" their specific content that writing and reading are not considered true curriculum. Rasinski and Padak (2004) call for reading and writing to be taught in an integrated fashion. They believe the best way to become a good writer is to read a lot, and the best way to become a good reader is to read a lot. They go on to say that all reading assignments should have a writing component and all writing assignments should have a reading component.

In the content areas, teachers develop a habit of teaching and lecturing around the reading. They view literacy instruction as a barrier to the transfer of content and would often rather "tell" the students what they need to know. Reading and writing should be developed in the curriculum as ways to explore the content. In a balanced and comprehensive approach, students consistently use reading and writing to explore and discover in the content areas. Teachers need to foster the development of confidence in students to glean information from and comprehend what they read. They will need these skills beyond the classroom when a teacher is not there to help them.

Precautions and Possible Pitfalls

 Literacy is not accomplished just within school. The schools are often involved with the students only during schools hours, and the resources students have access to generally are equally available. Once they leave the school, the playing field for learning becomes uneven. Your students go home to very different environments and areas of the community. Resources are not equally distributed, and some students have advantages that others don't.

Be careful to not call attention to students who appear more resourceful at the expense of those who don't have access to the same resources. The beautiful Internet information that one student brought to class may put the other students, without computer and Internet access at home, at a disadvantage. Some parents foster literacy in their children and others may not. Environment plays a big part in how prepared your students are when they walk into your class. Don't make your students pay emotionally for a situation they can't control.

Sources

Cassidy, J., & Cassidy, D. (2004). Literacy trends and issues today: An on-going study. *Reading and Writing Quarterly, 20,* 11–28.

Fitzgerald, J. (1999). What is this thing called "balance." *The Reading Teacher, 53,* 100–107.

Rasinski, T. & Padak, N. (2004). Beyond consensus—-beyond balance: Toward a comprehensive literacy curriculum. *Reading and Writing Quarterly, 20,* 91–102.

Strategy 44: Reexamine the nature and notion of "content literacy" and how it is reflected in your professional approach to literacy-related content activities in your classroom.

What the Research Says

Behrman (2003) examines content area literacy by observing a summer six-week high school biology class. The class features a problem-based instructional approach by examining and working with biology-related realistic scenarios that include a community component.

The community component requires students to spend a considerable amount of time outside of school interacting with community mentors and biology-related workplaces. Each scenario must be analyzed and acted on in a somewhat workplace-like procedure. Students were free to select any sources of information that would help them learn and respond successfully to the problems as problem-solving was stressed over information retrieval. This can best be described as "field-based learning."

Behrman (2003) found that students placed high reliance on human resources (mentors) and the Internet and limited their use of print media and sources. Behrman explains that the use of multiple literacies and varied print material calls for reexamining the definitions of content literacy and adolescent literacy in general. The limited instructional focus on traditional print-based literacy needs to be expanded to include multiple texts, including electronic, spoken, nonlinguistic, and other representations of meaning and knowledge.

Behrman's data sets included notes of classroom observation and events, instructional experiences with mentors at field sites, and interviews with students and the teacher. In addition, students provided end-of-the-course surveys and reviews of student project reports. Data were analyzed qualitatively.

Behrman (2003) found that, without a textbook, the class supported students in a rich assortment of literacy activities. Students sorted out digital and oral forms of content information to construct responses to project prompts and the authentic problems posed within the scenarios. The Internet was used far more than the class library of traditional print texts and other reference material. The author concludes by asking readers to rethink the primacy of print text in acquiring content knowledge.

Classroom Applications

It is common for teachers to help students learn to use and read traditional textbooks. However, more and more textbooks are taking a back seat to the oral transfer of information, the multimedia Internet, and other sources of information (television, radio, magazines). Most teachers are now aware of the problems and benefits the Internet provides. Textbooks in many classes have been reduced to use only for reference or a source of answers if a lecture is not totally understood. The biggest problem, when the textbook is no longer the primary source of information, is determining the validity and relevance of information from other sources. A second problem is outright plagiarism as students copy and paste Internet information into their papers.

The tip here is to extend the potentially limited scope of how content literacy is defined beyond the textbook. Many times when students are asked for their sources, they just say "I mostly used the Internet," indicating an absence of a human intellect in evaluating sources. They place a higher value on Web-based sources than text-based sources without carefully assessing the validity of the content.

Ongoing curriculum development is needed in all classes to reflect content-area learning in nonschool sources (nontextbook or other school material) and contexts. To further this idea, teachers need to consider how information is obtained in most workplace settings and use that information in curricular design, stressing how to move content learning beyond the traditional textbook.

How do you quickly find a site on the Internet containing useful information related to your classroom unit and at an appropriate grade level? One strategy is to simply use a search engine or a directory organized for teachers and children, one that also screens out sites inappropriate for children. You might begin with one of these locations:

- Yahooligans is a directory and a Web guide designed for children. Sites are appropriate for ages 7 to 12.
- Ask Jeeves for Kids is a directory and a search engine based on natural language. You simply type in a question, and it finds the best site with the answer. Sites are appropriate for use by children.
- Searchopolis is a directory and search engine organized for students in the elementary grades, middle grades, and high school.
- KidsClick! is a directory and search engine developed for kids by the Ramapo Catskill Library System.

A second strategy is to select one of several central sites for each subject area and explore the resources for use during Internet workshop. A central site is one that contains an extensive and well-organized set of links to resources in a content area. In a sense, it is like a directory for a content area: reading, math, science, social studies, or another topic. Most are located at stable sites that will not quickly change. As you explore the Internet, you will discover these well-organized treasure troves of information. They will become homes to which you will often return, and you will develop your own favorites. Here are a few examples of central content sites:

Science

Eisenhower National Clearinghouse—http://www.goenc.com

Science Learning Network—http://www.sln.org

Math

Eisenhower National Clearinghouse—http://www.goenc.com

The Math Forum—http://mathforum.com/

Social Studies

History/Social Studies for K–12 Teachers, CoreComm—http://home.core.com

Reading/Literature

SCORE Cyberguides to Literature—http://www.sdcoe.k12.ca.us/

The Children's Literature Web Guide—http://www.ucalgary.ca/

The Literacy Web—http://www.literacy.uconn.edu

Designing a specific activity could be your third step related to the learning goals of your unit, using a site you have bookmarked. The activity may be designed for several purposes:

- to introduce students to a site that you will use in your instructional unit;
- to develop important background knowledge for an upcoming unit;
- to develop navigation strategies; or
- to develop the critical literacies so important to effective Internet use.

It is important during this step to provide an open-ended activity for students, in which they have some choice about the information they will bring to the project. If everyone brings back identical information, there will be little to share and discuss during the activity session. You may wish to prepare an activity page for students to complete and bring to the Internet activity discussion, or you may simply write the assignment in a visible location in your classroom.

The potential for innovative approaches to Internet literacy are endless. Be prepared to teach your students to retrieve information in ways that will serve them well both inside and outside of your classroom while respecting intellectual property rights.

Precautions and Possible Pitfalls

⚠️ "I just don't have the time!" This is a common response for teachers who have not integrated the Internet into their literacy curriculum. There are usually two different explanations for this statement. Some teachers say they don't have time in their schedule; other teachers say they don't have time to learn new instructional strategies for using a complex tool like the Internet.

More sources of information are available to students than ever before. The textbook and the school library were once the extent of 95 percent of class research. Now information can come from anywhere. It would be a mistake to not help students sort and deal with the vast range and quality of content information out there. You can avoid many problems with plagiarism and related issues by embedding respect for intellectual property rights into your assignment and curriculum in general. By doing this, you will also help them become better writers and turn in more interesting papers for you to evaluate. Preparing children for their future is not an extra, it is central to our role as literacy educators.

Source

Behrman, E. (2003). Reconciling content literacy with adolescent literacy: Expanding literacy opportunities in a community-focused biology class. *Reading Research and Instruction, 43*(1), 1–30.

 Strategy 45: As a content teacher, learn to carefully select literacy instructional design principle that have been documented to improve comprehension of specific content, skills, and higher-order thinking.

What the Research Says

📚 Because of the difficulty many struggling middle school students have with science content area texts, Carnine and Carnine (2004) examined and discussed six aspects of instructional design incorporating literacy strategies. The goal was to integrate middle school science content and reading skills to increase levels of students' success. The investigation examined an approach that featured carefully selected vocabulary, word reading instruction, oral and silent reading with reading fluency practice as needed, and explicit instruction on comprehension strategies, such as retelling, concept mapping, and summarization.

Classroom Applications

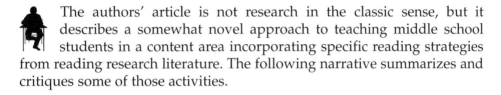 The authors' article is not research in the classic sense, but it describes a somewhat novel approach to teaching middle school students in a content area incorporating specific reading strategies from reading research literature. The following narrative summarizes and critiques some of those activities.

1. Students need good fluency before they can begin to concentrate on comprehension. In classes with a large number of struggling readers, oral reading fluency is highly correlated with and a predictor of reading comprehension. The fluency building activities and strategies recommended here involve rereading sections of previously read passages in order to build fluency. One of the best things about this technique is that students are able to graph their correct word-per-minute rate and see their improvement. Much of the time, progress in literacy activities is hard to see, but this technique helps provide real positive feedback visually. It may require a teacher to copy/retype and number passages from books previously read for students to use in this fluency exercise. Next, the cumulative number of words is noted in the left-hand column for each line. It is then simple for a student to keep track of the number of words read in one or two minutes. This is one of the most motivating activities when students can chart their own progress.

2. Students often have a difficult time and are confused and frustrated by the amount of new vocabulary and content thrown at them in school grade-level textbooks. It's hard to get the core or basic concepts in the midst of all the details stuffed into chapters. To strive for better comprehension, try carefully selecting key words, preteach them, and review them. You may need to decode and help the students pronounce these words also. Select the multisyllable words you think your students would have trouble with. Also begin to teach and define the meaning of prefixes, suffixes and affixes typical in such content areas as the sciences. All these are things you can do before reading assignments.

3. For comprehension strategies, try a "partner re-tell activity." Partner reading begins with the goal of identifying the main idea and

relating the details, actively engaging the pair of readers in the reading process. Partners trade the roles of "re-teller" and "listener" in short 30- to 60-second, face-to-face read-alouds. The re-teller recalls the main idea of his or her partner, who listens and relates to the re-teller. The next step is to have the pair focus on finding one or two details in the text that tell more about, support, and/or further define the main idea. In the end, the teacher can reinforce and confirm the important details or do a quick check on the activity with discussions and questioning. All this serves as a foundation for other activities to follow, such as some type of written work like content mapping.

4. The following are all part of an example of a scaffolding approach to teaching students to construct graphic organizers of the text they have read. This complex sequence of steps uses scaffolding to shift from teacher direction and control to student creation and then to student self-direction and control. This can be accomplished over time, within a variety of instructional units.

Show and explain to students a variety of traditional examples of graphic organizers, such as flowcharts, concept maps, and matrices, some developed by professionals and others by students.

Inform students about what graphic organizers are and when, why, and how various types of them should be used. Jones, Pierce, and Hunter (1988–1989) provide information on why and how to create graphic organizers to comprehend text; their article includes illustrations of a spider map, a continuum/scale, a series of events chain, a compare/contrast matrix, a problem/solution outline, a network tree, a fishbone map, and a human interaction outline.

As a classroom or homework assignment, give students a partially completed graphic organizer to structure. Give them feedback on their work. Have students complete empty graph organizers entirely on their own, and give them feedback on their work. Organize groups of students to create their own graphic organizers. Give students specific feedback on their construction and evaluation of graphic organizers, such as the following:

- The graphics are neat and easy to read.
- Ideas are expressed clearly.
- The content is organized clearly and logically.
- Labels or other strategies (colors, lines) are used to guide the reader's comprehension.
- Main or core ideas are the focus, not the details.
- The entire organizer is visually appealing.
- The reader doesn't have to turn the page to read all the words.

Once the groups complete their graphic organizers, have each group exhibit theirs to the other groups. Have all groups critique the graphic organizers of all other groups, giving creators feedback based on the rubric used. Supplement as necessary.

As a homework assignment, have students develop graphic organizers completely on their own, using rubric criteria. Encourage students to give one another feedback during the process.

Finally, have students work independently to create graphic organizers without support from others, either students and teachers.

Precautions and Possible Pitfalls

 In this era of testing content area, teachers are under increasing pressure to transfer content information students need to succeed on the tests. State frameworks and standards are defining specific class curricula more than ever. Some teachers decide to teach around reading problems and transfer the required information using other means.

Many times, teachers will see adding a literacy component as a threat to the limited time they have to teach their content. "Struggling readers" as a group include students who simply can't read (decode) text and others who are able to read but lack the necessary comprehension skills to reach grade-level expectations. The key for teachers is to incorporate strategies and instructional designs that address reading problems while, at the same time, facilitating content mandates.

Scaffolding is one of those teacher skills that will take time to develop. With experience you learn what type of support to provide and when to remove it. You need to make sure your scaffolding attempts are truly within your students' zone of proximal development. If the instruction is too easy, the work becomes "busy work." If it is too hard, no amount of scaffolding will help them perform independently and they will become frustrated.

Sources

Carnine, L., & Carnine, D. (2004). The interaction of reading skills and science content knowledge when teaching struggling secondary students. *Reading & Writing Quarterly, 20*, 203–218.

Jones, B. F., Pierce, J., & Hunter, B. (1988–1989). Teaching students to construct graphic representations. *Educational Leadership, 46*(4), 20–25.

Strategy 46: Consider popular song lyrics as a "prereading" vehicle to help create a motivating context for more specific subject matter concepts.

What the Research Says

Lloyd (2003) reflects on her experience with teenage students using lyrics and music from popular songs to represent perspectives rarely found in textbooks. She discusses how song lyrics can be used as textbooks in many disciplines to develop "critical literacy." Critical literacy, according to her research, is one application of critical theory, involving "reading the world," to understand how we as a society encode power structures and how and why knowledge and power are constructed. Within a reading pedagogy context, Lloyd describes using these lyrics as a "prereading" strategy." Lyrics as text work on a variety of levels to activate and build on prior knowledge of content in an academic context. The lyrics and the songs set the stage for further content reading in textbooks. The students' interactions with the lyrics are an example of the development of critical literacy.

Classroom Applications

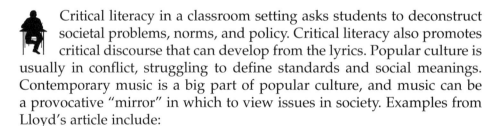

Critical literacy in a classroom setting asks students to deconstruct societal problems, norms, and policy. Critical literacy also promotes critical discourse that can develop from the lyrics. Popular culture is usually in conflict, struggling to define standards and social meanings. Contemporary music is a big part of popular culture, and music can be a provocative "mirror" in which to view issues in society. Examples from Lloyd's article include:

- Sting, "They Dance Alone": The lyrics describe a group of Chilean women who danced alone in front of government buildings with pictures of their missing husbands or sons, roughly 3000, who disappeared during the Pinochet era.

- Bob Marley, "Buffalo Soldiers" and "Get Up, Stand Up": "Buffalo Soldiers" was written to describe the Black soldiers of the nineteenth century, integrating the stories of freed slave histories. "Get Up, Stand Up" describes the injustice to Blacks in Jamaica.

- Woody Guthrie, "Dust Bowl Ballads": These lyrics describe the plight of marginalized migrant people and farmers.

- Rage Against the Machine, "Without a Face": The lyrics explore the plight of illegal immigrants coming across the border to look for work without any official status.

- Country Joe McDonald, "Fixin' to Die Rag," and Marvin Gaye, "What's Going On?": There are many antiwar songs and they are still being written today. Country Joe's anti-Vietnam War lyrics blame the government leaders and industry for the war. Marvin Gaye wrote his song in response to his brother's experience in the Vietnam War. Currently, Neal Young and Pearl Jam, among others, continue to add their voices to this genre.

- They Might Be Giants, "Your Racist Friend": The lead singer questions how his host at a party can stand by his racist friend.

- U2, "Sunday Bloody Sunday": Lyrics written by band member Bono, recall the events in Derry, Ireland, on January 30, 1972, when British soldiers and Irish Catholics clashed, resulting in 13 people dead and many others injured.

- Public Enemy, "Fight the Power": These lyrics provide social commentary on the state of racism. The song calls for people to resist the powers that subjugate Blacks and fight back through awareness.

These are just a few examples that could be used as triggers to look further into the curriculum. The beauty of song lyrics is that they are non-threatening "pop" poetry. Most people are familiar with many of the lyrics but haven't examined them from a scholarly perspective. Students will be more receptive.

Internet sites such as lyrics.com at http://www.lyrics.com/ and Song Facts at http://www.songfacts.com/ help define the lyrics and provide a range of information and opinion on certain song lyrics.

Precautions and Possible Pitfalls

 Exploring and deconstructing song lyrics may not seem like "real school" curriculum to some parents. Parents may not see lyrics in a curriculum as rigorous or formal enough. In addition, parents may see some songs/lyrics as "R" rated or worst. Always connect students with the radio version of lyrics you want to use.

Source

Lloyd, C.V. (2003). Song lyrics as texts to develop critical literacy. *ReadingOnline*. Available at: http://www.readingonline.org/

9

Literacy and
Instructional
Materials

Reading without reflecting is like eating without digesting.

—Edmund Burke

 ***Strategy 47: Use your school
hallways and other public areas
at school to display the use of a variety
of literacies as they provide insights
into how literacy is practiced and valued
(or devalued) in schools.***

What the Research Says

 Labbo, Montero, and Eakle (2001) explored a very overlooked
source of insight into literacy practices at schools by looking
at school hallways and other public spaces within schools.

A qualitative analysis of photographs of spaces in three elementary schools provided data to reflect on and assess how public display of literacy artifacts provide insight into a school's literacy practices. The forms and functions of things displayed on hallway walls reveal much about the school culture, what is valued, and what skills and tools are being utilized.

In this study, over a course of two weeks, the researchers took photos of all objects on the walls in three elementary schools. One rural, one suburban/urban, and one suburban school served as data sources. This was followed by a systematic analysis of the content of the photos. The researchers identified a number of categories of literacy artifacts:

Sense of community/identity: Literacy work products designed to foster pride, positive self-image, and a sense of school or community spirit

Curriculum/content area work: Literacy work products, individual or group, produced to illustrate the children's best efforts within a content discipline

Writing products: Displayed writing products including research reports, group compositions, poetry, and responses to literature

Author focus: Commercially produced posters and bulletin boards designed to promote reading or to provide information about authors

Functional signs: Basic signs providing directions, behavioral expectations, legal notices, or designations of how facilities are used

Conversely, the researchers also considered what was missing from the walls and what they thought should be included. They commented on materials and equipment left in hallways that was not intended for display and how that contributed to a view of the school environment.

Finally, after the study, they felt that little attention was being paid to the nature and the types of things that are posted in public display spaces in the school. They commented that very little of the space available was devoted to promoting multimedia literacies. It is their conviction that school public spaces can be additional valuable learning spaces to reflect and support multimedia literacy, especially if the school's cultural norms bend to accommodate time for pausing, wondering, reflecting, inquiring, and generally just noticing what's on the walls.

Classroom Applications

 If you are like many teachers, you have likely not given much thought to media representations exhibited in the hallways and common public areas of the school or their functions. You may have

noticed them but not in a context that provides insight into the role new media literacies play in schools. Items displayed in the hallways are a reflection of the media tools and communications strategies that are taught, used, and valued within the school's culture. How does this hallway evidence reflect on the multimedia literacy-based activities being integrated into classroom learning environments alongside the more traditional print-based literacies? One of the most interesting statistics in the Labbo, Montero, and Eakle (2001) study indicated that only 11 percent of the items displayed reflected use of computer-related tools.

The larger question for educators is how these public display areas can better be used to support students' active learning and foster development of new twenty-first-century media communications and other literacies. Here are a few ideas to consider:

1. Display the learning process, not just the final product. By focusing exclusively on the polished finished product, educators send a mixed message to students. Viewers' and children's learning could be enhanced by including a poster or photo essay describing the process needed to produce the final product.

2. Display multimedia computer-related work, not just paper and pencil products. If you are using computer time for skill-and-drill software applications, try expanding the uses to include Web-page design, multimedia presentations, computer art applications, photo manipulations, on-screen video production, multimedia slide shows, and other technology-driven media tools to "read" and "write" various symbolic forms of information (e.g., music, graphics, sound effects). Think about publicly displaying a computer screen in some way that can be seen in the public areas.

3. Don't use these spaces for storage. Using public space for purposes that are not instructional suggests overcrowded conditions or a lack of caring.

4. Don't leave wall space empty, or schools will look sterile and institutional, not like friendly places where young people can be stimulated to engage in learning. Try word walls of key instructional words, summaries of school events and participation, calendars or other concepts of time, activity lists, and theme-based bulletin boards designed to display the best students work. Display materials that invite celebration and also provide a literacy or communication activity challenge to those creating the display.

5. Set standards for spelling, grammar, and appearance of all exhibited work.

Precautions and Possible Pitfalls

 Public spaces within schools are limited resources. Encourage all members of the school community to utilize the space. Don't overlook student groups that traditionally do not engage in these types of activities. Participation in public exhibits builds the school community and engages students in ownership of the school experience. It also creates a learning environment that values student work and pride.

Source

Labbo, L. D., Montero, M. K., & Eakle, A. L. (2001). Learning how to read what's displayed on school hallway walls—and what's not. *Reading Online*, 5(3). Accessed on April 4, 2006, at: http://www.readingonline.org/

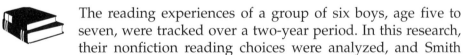 *Strategy 48: Help young boys make a positive and compatible connection between their masculinity and success as readers.*

What the Research Says

The reading experiences of a group of six boys, age five to seven, were tracked over a two-year period. In this research, their nonfiction reading choices were analyzed, and Smith (2004) identified ways in which the boys made positive connections between their masculinity and their reading. At the beginning of the study, the researcher was looking for the factors that are associated with successful young male readers and the nature of their reading experiences. One dominant factor associated with reading success the Smith study found was the development of a masculine identity that included, not excluded, reading. Four aspects of research looked at were the subject matter of the boy's reading, the dominance of sports in the boy's life, his advanced level of general knowledge, and the role of his father within the boy's reading choices.

Smith (2004) found that their nonfiction reading centered on typical boy interest areas and hobbies (soccer, space, dinosaurs). It was found that the boys became "experts" in some of these areas. According to the research, this earned them the respect of their peers, especially other boys, and a positive masculine identity in the classroom. Thus, being a successful reader and having a positive male identity became compatible. This study found reading was a desirable activity for boys in the sample group.

Classroom Applications

 In schools there are many ways of being a "boy." There are also many ways boys experience literacy. In some settings, when boys connect to reading or school achievement, they risk being seen as different by their peers. Some young people see reading as being more of a female activity. In a subtle way, boys can see themselves as subordinating their masculine status if they read successfully.

Teachers need to look for ways to better connect some student versions of masculinity with classroom instructional literacy goals and endorse them. Once these connections are made or available, engaging in instructional literacy activities can be acceptable, and even desirable for boys.

In the Smith (2004) study, the gender/reading compromise the boys made was to focus heavily on the stereotypical masculine interest areas of reading. Teachers made it a point to have these books available. The boys also exhibited stereotypical views on texts more suitable for male interests and also for female readers. It's clear their choices were socially and culturally influenced. One way to help them broaden the range of interests is to challenge their ideas and perceptions regarding masculine and feminine reading choices and help open their minds to a wider range of reading choices. With knowledge, boys can be encouraged to open up their reading choices. However, even if they don't accept this knowledge, keeping a genre of reading material that is acceptable and not threatening to a male's masculine sensibilities and identity is key.

While this was only one small study, it did produce tips and hints that could be very useful in many settings. Reading material needs to be carefully selected within the cultural and social constraints of your classroom, school, and community.

Don't forget to use the range of book lists out there to help in selecting books appropriate for your age group and their sensibilities. An Internet search will bring up many lists that can be used to help you and your students select books for the classroom, library, or home. The goal is to help young people find books they will enjoy and not threaten their social and peer group standing.

Precautions and Possible Pitfalls

Peppered throughout the educational research is perception that it is not always "cool" for males to be good students or readers in some settings. It would be a huge mistake not to very carefully evaluate and consider your students' demographics before stocking your library or classroom bookshelves. Many small student peer and cultural or racial groups need to be accommodated with appropriate reading material. Your selections can motivate or turn off and exclude any one of these groups.

Source

Smith, S. (2004). The non-fiction reading habits of young successful boy readers: Forming connections between masculinity and reading. *Literacy, 38*(1), 10–24.

 Strategy 49: Include multicultural works when developing a quality English curriculum.

What the Research Says

 Even with the widespread calls for more multicultural texts and literature in secondary English curricula, teachers have encountered roadblocks to integrating new literature into their courses. Selections do not always hold up well against competition from the great works of more traditional canons. In this context selected multicultural additions often are marginalized. Nontraditional authors do not fit comfortably into the curriculum.

Another concern is that students often distill a curricular march through the more classic selections as a search for "right" answers, with little connection to why the works were chosen or how they might connect to a larger purpose. The content has little or no context or connection to students or to other parts of the curriculum. Research seeks to discover a more "knowledge in action" discourse and current conversation about living traditions. The main concern is that lists of classics, or the selected tradition, predispose curriculum to a more teacher-centered and less student-centered pedagogy. A student-centered approach would strive to include multicultural texts as "curriculum in conversation" and use it as a framework for discussing multicultural literature.

In Burrough's (1999) research, three teachers' experiences were used as part of a larger study of teacher decision-making regarding curriculum involving eight English teachers in 19 classrooms in two high schools. The three teachers featured in the paper came from the same high school, which had a diverse student body with more than 50 percent African American students. Observations were taken over a two-year period as teachers worked, with varying degrees of success and motivation, to integrate multicultural literature into the curriculum.

Of the three experiences, one included very little multicultural curriculum because the structure of the teacher's course and her teaching style crowded it out. A second included many multicultural works and changing conversations that put multicultural curriculum at the center of instruction. Another teacher actually established a multicultural curriculum course and changed what were defined as literary works while creating new conversations to analyze them. She expanded what has been traditionally considered literature.

Classroom Applications

The task of creating a more multiculturally inclusive literary curriculum yielded three very different responses from the teachers in the study. Their responses also helped redefine and develop new ways of thinking about what curriculum is and how it should be selected. The research showed that changing to a more inclusive curriculum requires more than just selecting multicultural texts and a range of minority authors. While this is an essential and positive starting point, simply selecting is not enough. For example, teachers in this study expanded the term "literature" to include speeches, myths, plays, and journals, as well as novels and poems.

Beyond making selections, teaching and learning also require thinking about how teachers and students should experience and appreciate the content and its context. Scope and sequence were also seen as important, and the construction of "curriculum" needs to incorporate some intellectual continuity of discourse as a theme. Teachers in these studies found that the types of student conversations desired began to drive decision-making. They found students responded well to some selections and not to others. Adjustments were made. In the Burroughs (1999) study, the least successful teacher added only one multicultural text to her existing curriculum and students found little context and relevance in the scope and sequence of the course.

The major problem the teachers in the study encountered was the challenge of providing a scope and sequence without the class time and space. Teachers found that, unlike in a college course where literature can be more effectively grouped as a coherent curriculum, high school students lack the background and teachers have a difficult time making connections between time periods and source cultures. The literature range required for high school is too broad and time is too short.

One way two of these teachers solved the problem was to make textual selection criteria a more explicit part of the classroom conversation. One created a theme called "What Is American Literature," which allowed him to move away from a more traditional approach. In the new multicultural literature course, "World Cultures," the teacher created conversations to reflect cultural and individual differences within the classroom as well as within the literature. As teachers work to broaden the traditional literature canon, it is more realistic and useful to think about restructuring the entire curriculum rather than just adding a new text. Multicultural restructuring requires a look ahead as to how students will experience and use the new information they are given. Context and relevancy need to be considered, and strategies of discourse are very important. Although it was not mentioned in the research, the nature and makeup of each class can interact with curriculum in different ways. Diverse classes mean a variety and range of educational consumers, each with different expectations and mindsets.

Given an opportunity, the three teachers in this study responded to the challenge of inclusion with various degrees of motivation and success. What is clear is that inclusive curricular design is not easy. Giving a voice to traditionally marginalized groups is an art, not a science.

Precautions and Possible Pitfalls

Restructuring is always a process loaded with workplace politics over funding, department policy, priorities, and so forth. It would be a mistake not to begin to make the effort now because it will likely be mandated in the future. The only question individual teachers have to ask themselves is how are they going to respond to an inquiry about inclusion in their classrooms. They need to begin to develop a multicultural vocabulary when it comes to curricular discussions.

It is always a challenge for a teacher to replace curriculum. There are always worries that something taken out will be needed for a standardized test. Keep in mind that politics do play a part, and well-intentioned teachers can encounter resistance from all sides.

Sources

Agee, J. (2004). Negotiating a teaching identity: An African American teacher's struggle to teach in a test-driven context. *Teachers College Record, 106*(4), 747–763.

Burroughs, R. (1999). From the margins to the center: Integrating multicultural literature into the secondary English curriculum. *Journal of Curriculum and Supervision, 14*(2), 136–155.

Strategy 50: Take a look at one of the best resources for recommended literature available, the "Recommended Literature: Kindergarten Through Grade Twelve" on the California Department of Education's Web site.

What the Research Says

Grisham's (2002) article is not as much true research as it is a review of a great resource. Grisham spent time revisiting an old resource, cleaned-up and updated online at the California Department of Education's website. "Recommended Literature: Kindergarten Through Grade Twelve" was published first in 1989 at the height of literature-based reading programs in California. The original publication contained a list of children's books recommended for specific grade levels, categorized as "core" books to be used as whole-class readings, "recreational" for independent reading, and "extended" reading to build on core books. It was published again two years later in an annotated version with a short synopsis of each book on the list.

According to Grisham, California teachers generally found these resources highly useful for developing literacy strategies at the time, and school administrators found them indispensable as a reference for book adoptions for each grade level. As literacy instruction moved toward more skill-based programs the recommended literature list was not updated. However, in 2002 new technology produced an updated list online and the Web-based version has lots of features not found in the print version.

Classroom Applications

"Recommended Literature: Kindergarten Through Grade Twelve" is located on the California Department of Education's website at http://www.cde.ca.gov/. The following is a direct copy of the links and services they offer:

> Recommended Literature: Kindergarten Through Grade Twelve is a collection of outstanding literature for children and adolescents. The recommended titles reflect the quality and the complexity of the types of material students should be reading at school and outside of class.

Features:

Search List: Search the online database for titles using specific criteria.

Search Categories: Explanation of the search categories used in the online database.

Literary Genres: Explanation of the genres used in the online database.

Classifications: Explanation of the classifications used in the online database.

Awards: Explanation of and links to the home sites of the awards noted in the online database.

Connections to Standards: Gives background of content standards and how titles in the online database are linked to them.

Cultural Designations: Explanation of the cultural designations used in the online database.

District Selection Policies: Information about selection policies and Web resources.

Previous Literature Lists: Links to lists of authors and titles of previously published literature lists.

Frequently Asked Questions (FAQs): Answers to the questions most commonly asked.

Acknowledgments: A list of the many individuals who worked on this project.

The site is easy to navigate and is almost a "one-stop" website for literature searches. The search features and the links to book award sites are highlights of the site and a great resource for all educators. The powerful search engine breaks your search down by grade level, language, culture, awards, and a few other categories to really narrow your search boundaries. The Awards link searches many book award websites that are updated, and most also have links to past years' awards. These are two of the site's best features.

The California Department of Education has created an exceptional resource for the classroom teacher and others involved in literacy education.

Precautions and Possible Pitfalls

 There are none. There is very little not to like about this Internet site. The only potential problem might be that you might stop looking for other resources and depend on this site alone!

Source

Grisham, D. L. (2002). Recommended literature: A new children's literature resource. *Reading Online, 5*(9). Accessed February 28, 2006, at: http://www .readingonline.org/

 ### *Strategy 51: Use folk literature in the reading class.*

What the Research Says

 Folk literature, as Young, Bruchac, Livingston, and Kurkjian (2004) suggest, introduces students to many cultures, and it quickly becomes apparent that virtues such as honesty, hard work, mercy and forgiveness, gratitude, kindness, and learning are honored across cultures. For example, Harry Potter books feature a protagonist searching for important information about his heritage, who uses magic in his fights against evil. Teachers can also use nursery rhymes, fables, folk tales, literary tales, legends, epics and myths, and poetry related to folk literature.

Classroom Applications

 Terrell Young, Joseph Bruchac, Nancy Livingston, and Catherine Kurkjian (2004) suggest the following types of folk literature can be included in literacy classes:

Nursery rhymes: These include even the simplest tales because children can learn the elements of a good story from reading nursery rhymes. For example, they can learn about different types of characters, including main characters and subcharacters. They can also learn that a story must have a plot, setting, and theme. This knowledge will also help students in their later writing assignments.

Fables: Generally these are short stories featuring animal characters that teach young people lessons with stated morals, such as the now famous Aesop's Fables.

Folk tales: In the past, many of the great cultures of the world passed their values from one generation to the next through folk tales told in the form of brief oral narratives. Teachers of literacy should include such folk tales because they possess the following features: they have heroes and heroines, they outline plot lines, and they have unambiguous story lines with easily identified conflicts and resolutions that are usually decisive.

Literary tales: Young, Bruchac, Livingston, and Kurkjian (2004) observed that some authors choose to create new tales using traditional folk motifs and styles. These stories are referred to as literary tales because they are passed on through the oral tradition and written down by known authors, such as Hans Christian Andersen's literary tale, "The Ugly Duckling."

Legends: Legends share stories of the heroic deeds of historical figures, usually saints, kings, or heroes such as Robin Hood. Legends are also good reads for students in literacy classes.

Epics and myths: An epic is a long narrative or a cycle of stories clustered around the actions of a single hero. Epics grew out of or along with the myths, which contain messages to guide human behavior, are often considered sacred stories, and are the oldest stories.

Precautions and Possible Pitfalls

 Because there are many types of folk literature to choose from, teachers must be careful not to confuse their students with too much choice; they could possibly have a class read one genre of folk tale at a time.

Source

Young, T. A., Bruchac, J., Livingston, N. & Kurkjian, C. (2004). Folk literature: Preserving the storytellers' magic. *The Reading Teachers*, 57(8), 782–792.

 ### *Strategy 52: Let children read and write great poetry.*

What the Research Says

 Many literacy teachers struggle not only with the whole idea of teaching their students how to appreciate poetry but also with what kind of poetry to choose for their students to read. Janine Certo (2004) considered this issue when she asked herself if the poems used in literacy classes for young students not only challenge them appropriately but also enrich their lives. She decided that choosing "great" poetry could do both. Certo (2004) maintains that when students are exposed to great poems at an early age, they get a greater understanding of the language of the past, and teachers should trust their students to develop their own voice in their writing even though they will be reading the language of the past. She also suggests that students and the teacher co-construct poetry links or assignments from an original text that are different from a traditional writing prompt used in literacy classes. For example, instead of the usual pattern of the teacher reading a poem in class and having students write their own poem, teachers spend time in class helping students brainstorm ideas for writing their own poems by closely examining the poem the teachers chose to focus on.

Classroom Applications

Certo (2004) suggests that when selecting model poems for their students, teachers should avoid constant "sweetness themes" because students may already have the perception that poetry deals only with the topics of love or nature. In order to make students more aware of poetry with not-so-sweet themes, teachers should select a variety of themes that deal with other topics and issues. It is important the teachers themselves are excited about the choice of poem and if possible choose more than one poem that demonstrates the particular theme. If these poems are too long, then Certo (2004) suggests teachers can shorten them. In addition, teachers do not have to be overly worried if the vocabulary presented in these poems is difficult because this can be used to heighten the students' awareness of the language of the past. So it may be best to also choose poems that represent a variety of language styles.

When presenting these great poems to students, Certo (2004, p. 269) suggests taking the following useful steps:

1. Before reading the poem, outline the author's life briefly to humanize him or her, yet do not allow biography to override the author's work.

2. Follow the rhythm of the poem, reading it in a natural voice. (The physical appearance of most poems offers clues to the rhythm and mood of the words.)

3. Do at least two readings of the poem so students may further understand it and grasp its attractiveness.

4. After the poem is read, the teacher should be still and quiet without feeling pressured to ask children if they liked it.

5. After teachers model this process, students should have the opportunity to read the poem themselves.

Precautions and Possible Pitfalls

 The main pitfall with this method lies in the selection of the great poems. Just because the teacher is excited with the choice of poem this does not mean that the students will be equally excited. Also, the language style and the vocabulary levels of difficulty must be taken into consideration, and if these levels of difficulty are far above the students' current literacy levels, then the teacher will have a lot of work to do explaining the meaning of the text. However, this task can be greatly eased if teachers provide sufficient background about the poem: the author, the context, and the period when the poem was written. Teachers should bring in as much background material as possible to explain this clearly to their students so that they will have sufficient background knowledge before they read the poem.

Source

Certo, J. L. (2004). Cold plums and the old men in the water: Let children read and write "great" poetry. *The Reading Teacher, 58*(3), 266–271.

 ## Strategy 53: Use nonfiction readings in the primary grades.

What the Research Says

 Rosemary Palmer and Roger Stewart (2005) have observed that in the past many teachers and librarians steered primary-grade children into fiction rather than nonfiction reading because nonfiction books were perceived to be too difficult for young children to read by themselves. Now, however, they suggest that with nonfiction readers available for emergent readers, students can read books at their instructional reading levels and teachers can help them by using three models to structure their work with nonfiction: (1) teacher-directed instruction, (2) scaffolded student investigation, and (3) independent student investigation. The researchers maintain that the demands on students and teachers increase as teachers scaffold students through each model, starting with Model 1 and moving sequentially through the other two. Before teachers implement the models, however, Palmer and Stewart (2005) point out that students need to become familiar with nonfiction.

Classroom Applications

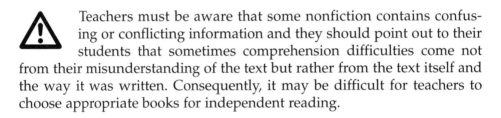 Palmer and Stewart (2005) suggest that a big book and class set of nonfiction titles are a good way to introduce this process, as the teacher sets a purpose for reading to help students access prior knowledge and experiences on a particular topic. Reading on the topic of frogs, Palmer and Stewart (2005) ask students "What do you know about frogs?" The teacher then writes facts on sticky notes, puts them on the chalkboard, and has the class organize the facts into categories they identify. Then the teacher helps the students generate questions, which become their purposes for reading. For example, to the question "Where do frogs live?" Palmer and Stewart (2005) suggest the teacher can model how to locate answers in the table of contents and index of a Big Book.

Precautions and Possible Pitfalls

Teachers must be aware that some nonfiction contains confusing or conflicting information and they should point out to their students that sometimes comprehension difficulties come not from their misunderstanding of the text but rather from the text itself and the way it was written. Consequently, it may be difficult for teachers to choose appropriate books for independent reading.

Source

Palmer, R., & Stewart, R. (2005). Models for using nonfiction in the primary grades. *The Reading Teacher, 58,* 426–434.

10

Family and Community Literacy

Children are made readers on the laps of their parents.

—Emilie Buchwald

 Strategy 54: Utilize a variety of print materials to inspire student reading and writing.

What the Research Says

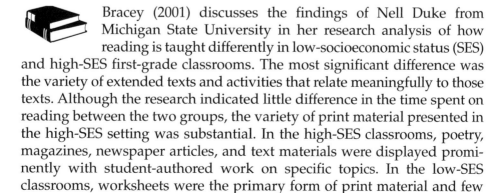 Bracey (2001) discusses the findings of Nell Duke from Michigan State University in her research analysis of how reading is taught differently in low-socioeconomic status (SES) and high-SES first-grade classrooms. The most significant difference was the variety of extended texts and activities that relate meaningfully to those texts. Although the research indicated little difference in the time spent on reading between the two groups, the variety of print material presented in the high-SES setting was substantial. In the high-SES classrooms, poetry, magazines, newspaper articles, and text materials were displayed prominently with student-authored work on specific topics. In the low-SES classrooms, worksheets were the primary form of print material and few

examples of extended student writing were present. Bracey also noted that low-SES school libraries had 40 percent fewer books available and seldom added to their numbers during the school year.

Classroom Applications

 Teachers need to ensure that the opportunity for reading a variety of print materials is available for their students regardless of grade level or content area. Research indicates that the more students read, the better their skills develop, and yet reading the standard classroom text often leaves students bored and unengaged, particularly if the text is outdated by student standards. Teachers need to use school librarians, the Internet, other teachers, parents, community members, and the students themselves to provide a wide range of print material beyond the basic textbook.

Many local newspapers have programs for free newspaper delivery to local classrooms. Often included with these papers are curricular activities that teachers can use or adapt to their own curricular needs. Many newspaper articles are short and provide a more motivating context for class content. Content and relevant "real-world" application for it will be more easily accessible for the struggling reader. Even comics and editorial cartoons provide opportunities for students to derive meaning from printed material.

Poetry and short stories abound on the Internet and can often be the perfect vehicle to introduce students to the elements of fiction in their own personal writing. Rhyme, rhythm, plot development, and characterization can all be addressed in context and act as a springboard for students as emerging authors.

Although worksheets may have their place in reinforcing rote memory skills, teachers would be wise to avoid relying on them as their number one way of infusing print material into their students' school day. Worksheets should be used as reinforcement rather than core curriculum. By providing a variety of print material, teachers can give students the opportunity to explore extended texts in meaningful ways.

Precautions and Possible Pitfalls

It is important that teachers remain mindful of school and district policy regarding materials that can be used in the classroom. Some districts allow anything and others have strict guidelines. Some districts have well-defined boundaries for acceptability of materials. It is very important that teachers make themselves aware of these policies prior to introducing controversial materials to their classrooms. Teachers should screen the materials they bring to the classroom to ensure they are appropriate for the students and the curriculum.

Source

Bracey, G. W. (2001). Does higher tech require higher skills? *Phi Delta Kappan, 82*(9), 715–717.

 Strategy 55: Encourage use of libraries to provide a more inclusive literature collection for sexual minorities.

What the Research Says

 Jones (2004) offers a number of suggestions to create a tolerant library environment that is respectful and supportive of sexual minorities. Libraries can compile articles, reports, and websites as well as fiction and nonfiction books to help adults and teens understand sexual minority issues and their effect on teen development. These teens have social, emotional, and health concerns that heterosexual teens don't. Jones feels that libraries should be safe, respectful, and tolerant environments that are supportive of diverse sexual identities. Libraries can provide resources that help teens understand diverse sexual orientations.

Classroom Applications

Just as teachers strive to provide a variety of resources that address different races, ethnic groups, cultures, religions, political beliefs, and so forth, they should make the effort to include sexual orientation as an aspect of diversity. Local and school libraries are often a valuable source of these materials. To help educators locate these resources, here are some online sites that support sexual minorities:

The Gay, Lesbian, and Straight Education Network (GLSEN) at http://glsen.org is an organization focused on safe and effective schools for diverse students.

Gay Straight Alliance Network at http://www.gsanetwork.org is an organization facilitating Gay Straight Alliance Clubs in schools.

Human Rights Campaign at http://www.hrc.org is the largest gay and lesbian organization.

Parents, Families and Friends of Lesbians and Gays at http://www.pflag.org is a site that promotes the well-being of sexual minorities.

Tolerance.org at http://www.tolerance.org is a project created by the Southern Poverty Law Center available to educators who might be interested in antibias issues and educational materials.

These websites provide a good place to start in selecting literature and other materials useful to sexual minorities and others interested in related topics.

Precautions and Possible Pitfalls

 It should come as no surprise that specific site and community politics exist in and around all schools. When new resources are introduced into the library, it is important that the administration supports the process. The last thing administrators want is to find out from an angry parent what is going on in the library. Libraries historically have been targets for censorship, and sexual orientation materials are often the major target.

Sources

Jones, J. (2004). Beyond the straight and narrow: Libraries can give gay teens the support they need. *School Library Journal, 50*(5), 45.

Swartz, P. C. (2003). Bridging multicultural education: Bringing sexual orientation into the children's and young adult literature classrooms. *Radical Teacher, 66,* 11–16.

 Strategy 56: Reflect on the complex issues surrounding school literature selection for bilingual and bicultural students.

What the Research Says

 Jones's study (2004) focuses on the questions of which strategies are the most appropriate in determining how literature is selected and how reading preferences for bicultural and bilingual students are identified. It also reflects on the potential negative consequences for bicultural and bilingual students of not providing literature that reflects their personal situation. The prime focus of the study is on data about students' reading choices, which are used to determine whether bilingual and bicultural students of inner-city Derby, Wales, can find their own identities within the literature they read. Is their identity split between their two cultures? Should bilingualism and biculturalism be seen as separate entities? Indian immigrants comprised the study group.

Jones then looked at minority publishing in Wales to explore the range of literature available. The goal was to identify positive steps teachers and schools could take in providing literature for bicultural and bilingual students that better connected to these students' backgrounds and intellectual needs.

Classroom Applications

When most students watch movies or read books, their own life experiences contribute to their enjoyment of the film or book. The more they share or identify with the characters or the situations presented, the more they like the book or movie. Conversely, the less affinity they have with the situations and characters, the harder time they have feeling empathy and enthusiasm. This is not always the case, but it helps if characters are dealing with situations the readers are familiar with in interesting and unique ways. Many people like to fantasize, placing themselves in the stories and wondering what they would do.

Students living in a bilingual or bicultural environment may have a tough time finding books or movies that deal with their life experiences. Where are the heroes they need to help shape their identity and give them their role models? Where are the books with gay and lesbian or bilingual and bicultural heroes? Chances are, most school libraries and classrooms select books more in tune with the experiences of the staff and faculty or the majority culture at the school. Also, much of the curriculum today is mandated or selected based on potential tests down the road.

Material that fits the needs of local minority populations is often hard to find and screen for appropriateness. School demographics are individual and localized. Today's schools are heterogeneous and it can be very difficult to standardize inclusive films, videos, and literature for all schools. This doesn't mean there is no need to address these concerns. Each site must make the effort to dig for the materials to meet the needs of its own student populations.

Precautions and Possible Pitfalls

Be aware that taking responsibility for more appropriate materials for these populations may not be popular. Funding the needs of minority groups can be a very political activity. School budgets are always tight. Most minority groups and their parents don't have the "political presence" to exert much power over those who control the funding. It will take individual teachers or staff advocates promoting these types of concerns to make a difference. Very often these caring individuals will also need to do the searching and research to help select the materials and argue for the funding.

Source

Jones, S. (2004). Shaping identities: The reading of young bilinguals. *Literacy,*
  38(1), 40–50.

 *Strategy 57: Find the "out–of–
classroom" forces that shape reading
habits and reading choices of young
people to better develop their personal
reading interests.*

What the Research Says

 Hopper (2005) considered the findings from data collected
during one week in May 2002 on the reading choices of 707
school children between 11 and 15 years old. The information
was collected in 30 schools in the southwest of England. The article reflects
on adolescent reading choices, influences on those choices, and the importance of profiling all reading experiences beyond books. This includes
"new" literacies such as the Internet, magazines, newspapers, comic books,
and other areas not typically considered traditional literacy activities.

Evidence from the study supported past research in that there has been
no significant decline in student literacy habits.

Classroom Applications

There is an intellectual gap between what teachers provide as
reading material and what young people choose to read, both in
class and for private reading. This can most likely be attributed to
a "generation gap." Teachers need to distinguish between promoting
curricular reading and fostering the students' personal reading interests.
The goal here should be to make the connections to the development of a
reading habit that will empower young people as learners and future citizens beyond your classroom curriculum. Being aware of how teens choose
their reading material will help you begin this journey toward offering
them a wide range of attractive choices for personal reading.

Giving students access to a range of appropriate reading books and
other literacy activities requires us to understand what triggers students'
choices. Hopper (2005) rates clear categories of factors affecting choice
that emerged from the study. Listed in descending order of importance,

these categories can provide insight you can use to foster your students' personal reading choices:

- Prior knowledge of the book or author
- The appearance of the book
- Recommendation
- Television or film
- Genre

Students often exchange information with others in their lives, creating a "prior knowledge" before deciding on a book to read. Prior knowledge connects with recommendations students might get from others. Young readers also read books as part of a series they might already be familiar with. This was a common response, as was reading multiple books from the same author. Genre choices, such a fantasy, were popular and specific interest in nonfiction subject matter was also mentioned, especially by boys. Current trends and detailed knowledge of available books students mention and also books in the same or related genre or by the same authors can be important.

The appearance of the book on the shelf also played a role in a student's decision to read. The color, pictures, or font could be a significant factor in choice. Publishers know this and create covers with images that affect the targeted demographic. The Harry Potter series is a great example of this. In addition, the same book might have different covers for different markets.

Television and film can also play a role, although a lesser one. The media hype certain books; again, the Harry Potter series as well as the Lord of the Rings got lots of media play. Oprah's Book Club influences choice, and sales jump for any book she recommends.

Genre is easy to connect to choice. Kids often become fans of a specific genre such as science fiction or sports. These two genres are safe choices for boys.

Regarding other forms of reading materials or nonbook sources (93 percent in Hopper's study cited reading nonbook text during the study week), girls spend more time reading magazines. You can see this in what students carry around with them at school. Girls show more interest in love, sex, celebrity, fashion, and health magazines, and boys show interest in technical, computer, and sports magazines. In the Hopper (2005) research, magazines proved to be an important reading choice for teens. Following magazines, newspapers were a significant nonbook reading source, and teens tended to read what was brought into their own households. Although not as popular as magazines or newspapers, the Internet was also cited as a source of nonbook reading.

Not surprisingly, teachers play a small role in influencing choice except for required class readers. This could be attributed to teachers' general lack of knowledge regarding what teenagers want to read.

So what do you do with this information? You use it to gain insight for stocking your own libraries or creating reading lists to share with your students. You can also use it to integrate more popular reading choices into your curriculum. You can use it to provide gender-specific choices to appeal to both boys and girls and to hard-to-reach groups of "nonreaders."

Precautions and Possible Pitfalls

 Developing an ongoing awareness of the reading preferences of teenagers takes time, and the job is never done. It's almost like predicting the type of music they are going to like. Many book lists online can help, and most are updated regularly. Just do an Internet "book-list" search and pick the lists that seem to be the most valid and useful, offer the greatest insight, and are the most current. There are also many agencies, clubs, and organizations that give book awards, and these are good sources of literary information. There is no one right way to develop this knowledge, but once you begin to tap into it you will be better able to inspire teens and expand the range of what literacy can be for them in a school setting.

Source

Hopper, R. (2005). What are teenagers reading? Adolescent fiction reading habits and reading choices. *Literacy, 39*(3), 113–128.

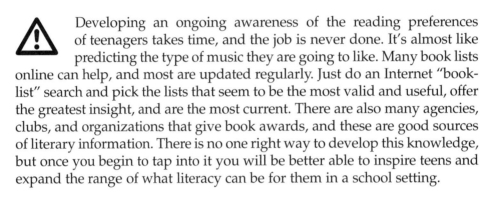

Strategy 58: Don't overlook the obvious, the public library and the library card, as motivating factors within your literacy strategies.

What the Research Says

 Two research efforts (Fisher Lapp, & Flood, 2001; Whitehead, 2004) looked at the effects of the students' access to print material through public library card ownership and class trips to the local community library. Reading performance, attitudes toward reading, time spent reading at home, number of books at home, and family visits to the library after school were compared between students who had library cards and students who didn't have library cards. In addition, the research included more informal individual visits to the public library, which became a research variable.

The research asked whether children who had library cards and checked out two to four books a month with their class would

1. Spend more time reading at home?
2. Have better attitudes toward reading?
3. Perform better in the area of reading comprehension?
4. Visit the library more with their family?

This research took place in a large urban high school district. The study site was an inner-city school in San Diego, California, with 93 students from five second-grade bilingual classrooms. One of the classes had been going on trips to the public library twice a month for a total of 12 visits. Three of the five went on field trips to the library for a total of eight times, and a single class, acting as a control, never went to the library during the school year. All students were Hispanic and native Spanish speakers. All students had at least basic literacy skills in Spanish and a range of literacy skills in English. These students all lived in the same community with close proximity to both school and a public library.

The results of the study were as follows:

- Students with library cards read at a 23 percent higher rate and spent 14 more minutes reading than those without cards.
- Students with cards reported having 23.5 book titles at home compared to 20 in homes without cards.
- Students without cards also reported visiting the library 50 percent less frequently.
- Students without cards reported the lowest average time spent reading at home.
- A district-approved developmental reading assessment indicated a one level lower score for students without cards.
- Students with library cards had higher averages in every area of measurement in this study.
- The only area of the study that supports previous research and expectations is that students who did not go to the library exhibited greater satisfaction in reading compared with those who went to the library.

Classroom Applications

 Some of the conclusions of this research seem obvious, and this study supports most other research on the subject.

- When students read voluntarily, their reading improves.
- When students have easy access to books, they read more.

- When students who own library cards visit the library as a class, they have more access to print.
- The Fisher and coworkers (2001) study showed a range of 53 to 95 percent of the students with cards felt themselves to be "a good reader."

The mandate is clear for teachers; they need to facilitate access to print material in any way possible and also provide opportunities for students to read. Consider the following questions about utilization of resources in your setting:

- Is it possible to use the local public library as a class or offer academic reinforcement for owning library cards and using the library?
- Is it possible to make more use of the school library or offer reinforcement for using the school library?
- Can you as a teacher begin to collect and offer relevant reading material in your own classroom for student checkout?
- Can you offer some kind of reward or grade consideration for voluntary reading?

The last result, listed in the Fisher (2004) study, appears to be the most interesting for teachers. When 53 to 95 percent of the students feel they are good readers, what opportunities and power does a teacher have to build or lower the confidence level of a student in areas of his or her academic performance? What can a teacher do to enhance literacy development and instruction in general? Further, while this study focused on elementary school age students, how can its results be relevant for high school age students?

Last, in this era of high-stakes testing, children who read more were shown to outperform those who do not on a variety of standardized assessments. On the California mandated SAT-9, students with higher access to print material had increased performance of 21 percent "at or above grade level" compared to a control group that only exhibited a 4 percent increase (Fisher, Lapp, & Flood, 2001).

Precautions and Possible Pitfalls

 Offering rewards and incentives for "outside-of-class" visits to the library could create an uneven playing field for your students. Not all students have the family support necessary to provide them with the opportunity for library visits. Once leaving your classroom, learning resources are not equally available to everyone. You may be giving an unfair advantage to some students with greater access to learning resources outside school. There are few easy answers here.

Sources

Fisher, D., Lapp, D., & Flood, J. (2001). The effects of access to print through the use of community libraries on the reading performance of elementary students. *Reading Improvement, 38*(4), 175–182.

Whitehead, N. (2004). The effects of increased access to books on student reading using the public library. *Reading Improvement, 41*(3), 165–178.

Strategy 59: Literacy programs work best by involving the whole family.

What the Research Says

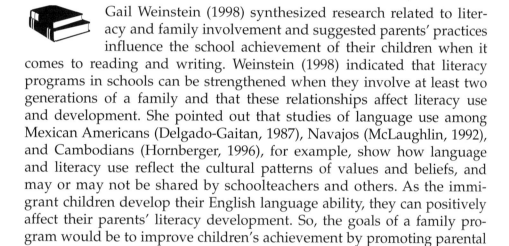

Gail Weinstein (1998) synthesized research related to literacy and family involvement and suggested parents' practices influence the school achievement of their children when it comes to reading and writing. Weinstein (1998) indicated that literacy programs in schools can be strengthened when they involve at least two generations of a family and that these relationships affect literacy use and development. She pointed out that studies of language use among Mexican Americans (Delgado-Gaitan, 1987), Navajos (McLaughlin, 1992), and Cambodians (Hornberger, 1996), for example, show how language and literacy use reflect the cultural patterns of values and beliefs, and may or may not be shared by schoolteachers and others. As the immigrant children develop their English language ability, they can positively affect their parents' literacy development. So, the goals of a family program would be to improve children's achievement by promoting parental involvement.

Classroom Applications

This is a unique opportunity for teachers to "bring" the community into the classroom, encouraging the parents to visit their literacy lessons and participate in discussions and language-development activities. A major objective of a family literacy program is to improve reading skills (Weinstein, 1998), and this can be achieved when the teacher provides a variety of reading activities such as teaching parents to imitate behaviors of parents in the homes of successful readers such as reading aloud to children and asking them specific questions. The children can also reverse this process by reading aloud to their parents when they return home from school. This becomes a two-way instruction program with parents sometimes teaching their children and the children sometimes teaching their parents. In this way, generations can reach out to each other.

One example of such activities in action is getting the different generations of one family together in the classroom to discuss their family, backgrounds, beliefs, and values and how these compare with what they see in their community. The teacher can help prepare for this by gathering information about the family's cultural background from magazines and books. For example, if the children are from a country in South America, the teacher can access photos of the family's country of origin from *National Geographic* and other sources and videos about life in that country and then get the elders to describe the photos and explain the videos to the children in the class. In this way, both generations get practice in a range of literacy skills while passing knowledge from one generation to another.

The class can produce a booklet on the culture in focus, and/or develop a webpage on various aspects of that family's life such as a family tree. This project-based work can link the classroom to the wider community and better involve parents and their children in developing literacy skills although the focus is not on language learning.

Precautions and Possible Pitfalls

 The main problem in setting up intergenerational literacy programs is "selling" their worth to both generations. The parents need to be informed about the benefits, especially the language and literacy benefits, of participating in such a nonlinguistic project. The children need to be informed about the benefits of the two-way language instruction program that lie behind such a method. When the teacher informs both sides about the benefits of this two-way intergenerational method, the family project can progress smoothly.

Sources

Delgado-Gaitan, C. (1987). Mexican adult literacy: New directions for immigrants. In S. R. Goldman & K. Trueba (Eds.), *Becoming literate in English as a second language* (pp. 9–32). Norwood, NJ: Ablex.

Hornberger, N. (1996). Mother-tongue literacy in the Cambodian community of Philadelphia. *International Journal of the Sociology of Language, 119,* 69–86.

McLaughlin, D. (1992). *When literacy empowers: Navajo language in print.* Albuquerque: University of New Mexico Press.

Weinstein, G. (1998). *Family and intergenerational literacy in multilingual communities.* ERIC Q&A. Washington, DC: National Center for ESL Literacy Education.

Strategy 60: Explore ways parents can help their children read at home.

What the Research Says

 Research (e.g., Darling, & Westberg, 2004) indicates that parent involvement has a positive influence on student achievement, especially in terms of literacy acquisition, and that even active parent involvement in their children's education at home has a more significant impact than when teachers try to engage their students in learning in school activities. This research also indicates that early literacy behaviors in reading, such as knowledge of letter names and letter sounds, phoneme awareness, and early decoding abilities, as well as word recognition and reading comprehension, can be enhanced when parents get involved with their children's literacy development.

Classroom Application

 Literacy teachers can encourage parents to become more involved with children's literacy and thus make their classroom job easier by asking parents to attend some workshop (training) sessions that teach them how to achieve this task at home. Reading teachers can train the parents to be involved by teaching them how to listen correctly to how their child reads at home and give corrective feedback. Each literacy teacher can thus enhance his or her classroom instruction by involving the parents with backup literacy activities in the home, specifically teaching them what they should do rather than leaving it to chance. This creates a greater connection between school work and homework.

Precautions and Possible Pitfalls

 Of course, parents have been listening to their children read and may think they do not need any specific literacy training to do this at home. However, research indicates that training parents to teach their children reading with specific exercises produced greater results than if teaching were left to chance. Teachers should thus make specific plans that are comprehensible to parents and conduct follow-up workshops to ensure they are doing what the teacher suggested. Teachers themselves should be clear about what they will teach the parents and want the parents to accomplish.

Source

Darling, S., & Westberg, L. (2004). Parent involvement in children's acquisition of reading. *The Reading Teacher, 57*(8), 774–776.

Strategy 61: Make children aware of community library literacy programs.

What the Research Says

Eileen McMurrer and Lynda Terrill (2001) observed that, over the years, individual states and communities have continued to fund projects to reach diverse local populations in their communities; for example, from 1988 to 1995 the California State Library funded the Partnerships for Change Program, which involved 26 community libraries, analyzing and restructuring programs and policies to better serve their culturally diverse communities. They discovered that libraries provide literacy services in one or more of three forms: they develop collections that support existing literacy programs; they partner with existing literacy programs; or they provide literacy programs either inside the library or in other locations.

Classroom Applications

Literacy teachers can become more involved in these library literacy programs by providing the library nearest their school with facts concerning the children in their classrooms. For example, if a school discovers that their school community is ethnically diverse with, say, Vietnamese and Cuban populations, then the teacher can suggest the library add small collections of materials in Vietnamese, Spanish, and English for nonnative speakers. In this way, the teacher can make sure that the materials do not negate the children's native language while trying to promote English literacy but, in fact, promote the positive role literacy in the native language can play with children learning English.

The literacy teacher can also try to expand this program by attempting to connect with other community agencies that deal with immigrants, such as bilingual outreach centers, and then set up a network among the school, the library, and the outside community. This can be coordinated on the Web from one source, the school, and the children can also be encouraged to get involved in the program by posting comments on the library literacy program both in their native language (not only for parents not yet literate in English to read, but also so as not to lose their native language) and in English (for the teacher, the library, and the community at large to read).

Precautions and Possible Pitfalls

 It may not be easy for the teacher to incorporate learners' languages into instruction because of the wide range of languages possible in any one classroom. Furthermore, it may be equally difficult to monitor what is said or written in the children's native language. Therefore, it may be necessary to involve the parents as a language source from the very beginning by getting the library to connect adult literacy programs to these new children literacy programs. The next strategy addresses the issue of using a child's native language in literacy instruction.

Source

McMurrer, E., & Terrill, L. (2001). *Library literacy.* ERIC Q&A. Washington, DC: National Center for ESL Literacy Education.

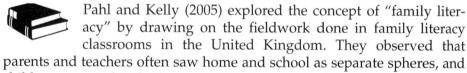

Strategy 62: Rather than imposing a school literacy curriculum upon parents, consider listening to the parents' voices about a shared curriculum.

What the Research Says

 Pahl and Kelly (2005) explored the concept of "family literacy" by drawing on the fieldwork done in family literacy classrooms in the United Kingdom. They observed that parents and teachers often saw home and school as separate spheres, and children operated in both spaces. Their research defines a "third space" between home and school. The study centered on younger children and examined various parents/child/literacy interactions in family literacy classrooms.

In this work, a family literacy classroom is described as a place where educators attempt to join home and school by focusing on shared literacy activities with parents and children, usually practiced on school sites, drawing on home-based activities. Family literacy classrooms are seen as a place, between home and school, were both home and school literacy realms are recognized and validated. They serve as a third space where particular types of texts and discourses are produced. Usually this is seen as literacy activities from home being linked to school curriculum.

Various practices were examined in this context, exploring how these family literacy classrooms can act as places where children's texts can move from home to school and back again.

Classroom Applications

This application offers ideas and not a specific program or practice. In the large framework of parental involvement in schools, the idea of creating a "class" where parents and their students can interact is unique. The idea can trigger brainstorming on how the concept might work in a variety of settings and focusing on a number of purposes. Pahl and Kelly (2005) explored a number of these classrooms where parents and students come together with teachers.

Most of the participants in these classrooms were students and their families who came from bilingual, bicultural households. All the programs examined targeted early elementary or preschool students. Most had multilingual identities that were upheld, validated, and recognized in these programs. In most settings, these are the parents that participate in school programs the least. This is what makes the idea of a family literacy classroom most appealing. Parents were encouraged to draw on multiple languages and cultural perspectives to produce various products or artifacts within the activities and curriculum of the class.

Beyond the more traditional curriculum, the idea of a class where parents and students come together to spend time together talking, sharing, creating, playing, reading, writing, listening, and laughing is appealing! Pahl and Kelly noticed (but did not quantify) that many of the children's skills, knowledge, understanding, and confidence grew, and the parents' self-esteem grew as confidence in speaking in groups and risk-taking improved. Parents were better able to ask for information and share ideas and felt better able to approach the school. Standards in reading, writing, spelling, and use of grammar also improved.

So how can you use these examples and information? As every school setting is different, any opportunity this concept provides has to be considered individually and crafted by motivated educators. Many schools have a problem involving bilingual, bicultural families, and this idea offers possible solutions. This problem is especially prevalent in the older grades. The opportunities a family literacy class can provide are limited only by your imagination! They may also require a paradigm shift in educators regarding what family involvement in schools can look like.

Precautions and Possible Pitfalls

Parents work or don't always want to be involved in schools. The lack of parent participation in your program can create an uneven playing field for some students, both academically and emotionally. You will need to consider children of both participants and nonparticipants. What can you do to compensate students of nonparticipants? There are no easy answers, but you will need to consider the issues involved.

Source

Pahl, K., & Kelly, S. (2005). Family literacy as a third space between home and school: Some case studies of practice. *Literacy, 39,* 91–96.

 Strategy 63: Become an advocate for improved home literacy environments (HLE) for all students, especially for preschool and K–3 students.

What the Research Says

 Burgess (2002) uses a research approach to further define what is obvious to most educators: shared reading experiences in home environments relate to the development of phonological sensitivity and oral language skills in young children. Informal literacy acquisition is thought to start at an early age, long before the child enters the formal classroom. The time children spend with parents early in their development is seen by most as key to their preparation for school-based, more formalized instruction.

The results of Burgess's study indicate that shared reading experiences (parents teaching children to read words or reading to their children) relate to language outcomes in oral language composition, expressive and receptive vocabulary, and phonological sensitivity. This study looked at the literacy environments of 115 four- and five-year-olds from middle-income homes through parent surveys recording shared reading patterns over time. Children completed two standardized tests of oral language and four tests of phonological sensitivity.

This is one of the first studies to demonstrate a relationship between phonological sensitivity and shared reading and deficits in phonological sensitivity, which, according to Burgess (2002) and Wagner, Torgesen, and Rashotte (1994), are the most significant factors for most children having difficulties learning to read. Burgess goes on to state that the earlier children learn to read, the greater number of shared reading experiences they have.

Classroom Applications

If you are involved with preschool children or K–3 students, the research described here is for you. With the growing demand for parental participation, there is an increasing and widespread call for parents to read more to their children. Changing the home literacy environments is not easy. While the research does define the connections between home literacy environments and school literacy achievement, it doesn't define the specific activities that have been shown to improve reading-related skills. However, by facilitating literacy activities at home you can't go too far wrong.

Because not all household are rich in resources, you may want to consider lending libraries or some other means to get books into the hands of parents. You may also want to consider copying reading material to send home (remember to learn and respect copyright laws on educational use).

Precautions and Possible Pitfalls

 Most of the research on emergent literacy has been conducted with children from print-rich homes who identify with the dominant, school-oriented culture, where parent-child interactions provide experiences similar to classroom interactions. Through these experiences, children are motivated to learn about literacy events, functions, artifacts, forms (e.g., sound and letter names), and conventions before they learn more formally to read and write.

There is another side to this. There are reasons why parents may not want to read to and with their children. Maybe the parents are not comfortable reading aloud or they do not have access to reading and/or other literacy materials such as the Internet. Bilingual or bicultural students may have parents who are not English speakers. While the research doesn't describe these situations directly, some believe that literacy skills in one language contribute to literacy skills in other languages.

Finally, at school the educational resources are usually equally available to all students. Once students leave school, that is not the case. Some households offer greater opportunities for their children. Involving parents can produce an inequality among students, and educators need to be sensitive to children with home situations that are not optimal.

Sources

Burgess, S. (2002). Shared reading correlates of early reading skills. *Reading Online*, International Reading Association, Inc. Posted March 2002 at: www.reading online.org

Wagner, R. K., Torgesen, J. K., & Rashotte, C. A. (1994). Development of reading-related phonological processing abilities: New evidence of bi-directional causality from a latent variable longitudinal study. *Developmental Psychology, 30*, 73–87.

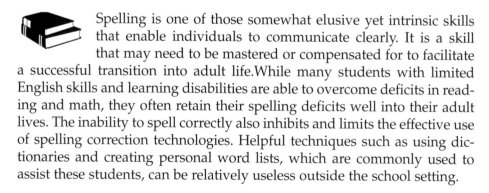

11

Literacy, Technology, and the Internet

A writer only begins a book. A reader finishes it.

—Samuel Johnson

 Strategy 64: Optimize the purchase and use of word-processing spell-checker programs to better serve the needs of students with learning disabilities.

What the Research Says

Spelling is one of those somewhat elusive yet intrinsic skills that enable individuals to communicate clearly. It is a skill that may need to be mastered or compensated for to facilitate a successful transition into adult life.While many students with limited English skills and learning disabilities are able to overcome deficits in reading and math, they often retain their spelling deficits well into their adult lives. The inability to spell correctly also inhibits and limits the effective use of spelling correction technologies. Helpful techniques such as using dictionaries and creating personal word lists, which are commonly used to assist these students, can be relatively useless outside the school setting.

Researchers Coutinho, Karlan, and Montgomery (2001) and MacArthur, Graham, Haynes, and De La Paz (1996) examined the use of spell-checkers in the context of word processing. Spelling instruction must not include only acquisition skills and remedial instruction to overcome the spelling deficit but also compensation skills and instruction that enable the student to write with accurate spelling. One popular compensation tool for writing is a word-processing program. Students need to become competent users of these programs and their features (e.g., spell-checkers) that will enable them to compensate for spelling weaknesses. Spell-checkers provide target words for misspellings based on keyboarding and spelling rule application errors.

Unfortunately, for a spell-checker to be useful for students with spelling deficits, it needs to provide the correct spelling for complex misspellings. According to the researchers, the spelling errors of students with learning disabilities are more complex than simple typos and rule application errors. Typical misspellings generated by such students can often be classified as severe phonetic mismatches, which have few phonetic characteristics similar to the target word. Often spelling choices appear less mature and may contain characteristics of younger children's errors.

With these factors in mind, researchers Coutinho and associates (2001) and MacArthur and coworkers (1996) surveyed a range of word-processing programs to identify those that serve the students most successfully. To accomplish this, they addressed three questions relating to the use of spell-checkers:

- Do the various spell-checkers provide the target word for misspellings first in the replacement list?
- Do the various spell-checkers generate the target word first in the replacement list equally across phonetic developmental level?
- Do the various spell-checkers generate the target word first in the replacement list equally no matter what proportion of correct letter sequences (bigram ratio) the misspelling contains?

For this study, a search of software catalogs identified nine word-processing packages that were designed for school use and included spell-checkers. Two of the nine programs (Write This Way and Write Outloud) were designed specifically for students with disabilities. In addition, two word-processing packages commonly used in college and university settings (WordPerfect 5.2 for Windows and Microsoft Word for DOS 6.0) and two word-processing programs commonly sold with computer packages (Microsoft Works 4.0 and Claris Works 4.0) were included.

Classroom Applications

Because the range of students with spelling deficits is highly variable, no single program is going to be the answer for everyone. As technology continues to develop at an amazing speed, teachers will need to continue to update their information regarding what works for their specific students in the context of the individual classroom. The best suggestion that comes out of this research is that spell and grammar checkers are important. Teachers should consider the software's checkers for all student groups before making a final decision. This is especially true for students with learning disabilities. Ease of use and the students' range of ability levels are also important considerations in making a final evaluation.

Precautions and Possible Pitfalls

 Regardless of the software selected, it is essential that teachers take the time to become proficient with the application, including becoming familiar with the various tools it offers to facilitate student use. It's always a good idea to contact colleagues who may be experienced with the software, and don't forget to access company help lines as needed.

Sources

Coutinho, M., Karlan, G., & Montgomery, D. (2001). The effectiveness of word processors' spell-checker programs to produce target words for misspellings generated by students with learning disabilities. *Journal of Special Education Technology, 16*(2), 27–41.

MacArthur, C. A., Graham, S., Haynes, J. A., & De La Paz, S. (1996). Spelling checkers and students with learning disabilities: Performance comparisons and impact on spelling. *Journal of Special Education, 30,* 35–57.

 Strategy 65: Become just as familiar with literacy-useful software as you are with your students' favorite literature.

What the Research Says

 This research takes place within a kindergarten classroom and deals with five- and six–year-olds. The article describes how a kindergarten teacher and a university-based research collaborator used data from classroom observations to connect computer-related literacy activities to a variety of their students' literacy needs. They were looking for ways to better connect computer activities to the everyday routine of classroom life. The study looked at two students out of a kindergarten classroom drawn from a larger study set of 21 case studies. These two case stories were a small sample that would provide direction on how to utilize and integrate a small computer center into literacy activities.

The research weaves together the two case study narratives from qualitative data that include field note observations, interviews, journal notes, descriptions of the children's interactions with the computers/software, transcriptions of children's talk and printouts of students' work. This was combined with literacy assessments administered three times during the academic year. The classroom computer center consisted of three computers.

The researchers observed that many children with low literacy abilities were not benefiting from interacting with the technology designed to provide them with practice on literacy skills (e.g., alphabetic order, letter identification, sound-symbol relationships). Much of the time the children's time was spent playing the games but not learning. Some students were defined as "window shoppers," looking but not participating with the computer center. Others engaged in "mouse wars" as impatient waiters expressing all types of behaviors designed to gain control of the mouse.

The researchers went on to define the major problems with the computer center. They then presented a dialogue describing a shift toward positive interaction as different approaches to focusing and designing computer-related activities were tried.

Classroom Applications

First, the computer center described in the Labbo and Sprague (2000) study began its life as a side venture that was technically not part of the curriculum. While literacy-based software was installed on the computers, the students' main focus was on using the software for its "game" value, not its teaching and learning value. The computer center was used passively, and had no real connection to the general curriculum or other class activities.

Slowly the teachers began to connect instructional activities to the computer center. Once low-literacy-ability students found or were given a concrete purpose for the programs available at the computer center, they were able to extend their more mainstream literacy activities in the computer center.

Over the course of the year, the teachers discovered that a classroom computer center fit wonderfully into the instructional scheme. It worked best when the teachers found a way to use the technology to support thematic units and literature-based activities that occurred within the general instruction. Teachers became as familiar with the computer programs and their potential as they were with other literature within the curriculum.

The message here is that technology does not stand alone as an instructional tool. It needs to be integrated as an important element within other curriculum and instructional strategies. Make sure your connections are relevant and important to the overall lesson. For example, Labbo and Sprague connected Hutchins's *The Wind Blew* to the software program Kidpix Studio Deluxe, an art program, and to wind and wind-blown objects. Students created a computer picture and a story about things that blow in the wind. During a unit on jobs and careers, students were given the opportunity to design and make a business card. Students were asked to bring with them a children's book with career-related objects in the illustrations and text-based themes that could be used on the card. These are just two examples of how to integrate technology beyond its game or entertainment functions.

The following software programs were used in the study:

- Dr. Seuss's ABC (1995). Novato, CA: Broderbund Software
- KidPix Studio Deluxe 4 (1994). Novato, CA: Broderbund Software
- Jump Start Kindergarten (1997). Torrence, CA: Knowledge Adventure
- Just Grandma and Me (1997). Novato, CA: Broderbund Software

Precautions and Possible Pitfalls

 Students have to be taught how to use technology along with the curricular concepts. Don't underestimate the added responsibility of teaching the necessary skills. Not all children come from homes with computers and other technology, and you may be creating an uneven playing field where some children have advantages at home with prior experience that others haven't had.

Source

Labbo, L. D., & Sprague, L. (2000). Connecting a computer center to themes, literature, and kindergartner's literacy needs. *Reading Online*, International Reading Association, Inc. Accessed February 28, 2006 at: www.readingonline.org

 Strategy 66: Look to children's "out-of-school" uses of the Internet for instructional literacy strategies for the classroom.

What the Research Says

 Burnett and Wilkinson (2005) enthusiastically comment on all the new possibilities for engaging with information that is associated with a wide variety of literacy practices. Their study

explores the purposes for which young children, with routine availability, access the Internet, the attitudes and orientations they demonstrate in their approach to Web-based texts, and what has enabled them to develop as Internet users. The focus of the study was out-of-school uses. Their findings are used to make suggestions for supporting and framing the literacy uses of the Internet. They define "reading" Internet and digital texts as functionally distinct from print-based text, as decoding text, moving images, still images, sounds, and words. Meaning is created in different ways.

Their study focused on six-year-olds, three boys and three girls from a small rural primary school. Individual and whole-group interviews were conducted over a six-week period focusing on key questions regarding Internet use to gather the following information:

1. Reasons why children used the Internet

2. Descriptions of the sites they liked and visited

3. Advice for the students on how to access these sites

4. General reflections on skills needed to be effective Internet users

5. Experiences that had been significant in enabling them to become users

The researchers found the students' reasons for using the Internet were diverse. The most common were as a source of free stuff such as games, for downloading music, images, and so on, to enter into special interest communities for shared interests and enthusiasts, and to communicate with the world around them. The researchers end by offering suggestions on how to use this knowledge in the school setting.

Classroom Applications

Students rarely see the use of the Internet as "literacy" or learning activity. Their agendas are usually very "un-school"-oriented. As Burnett and Wilkinson (2005) found, the most common outcomes of Internet use for younger students were accessing free stuff such as games, music, and images, and sharing in special-interest communities. As students get older, e-mail and research for school activities become focuses. Veteran teachers of students in the upper grades know the educational pitfalls of easy access to questionable information. Because of such pitfalls, younger students can really use help using Web information appropriately. This is where the Internet can become the focus of literacy-based school activities in the younger grades.

The Internet is an ideal mechanism for encouraging students to assume responsibility for their own learning and build on and improve skills some have already developed. As students find different learning resources on the Internet, they become active participants in their quest for knowledge and information. Incorporating the Internet into your classroom provides students with more opportunities to structure their own explorations and, hopefully, learning. Once trained, students are able to define their learning needs, find information, assess its value, build their own knowledge base, and engage in discourse about their discoveries. Yet before you and your students can begin to use the Internet in your classroom, students need the foundation of two main sets of skills to help them navigate the Internet and manage the large amounts of information they find.

People rarely read webpages word by word; instead, they scan the page, picking out individual words and sentences. In a recent study, Morkes and Nielsen (1998) found that 79 percent of their test users always scanned any new page they came across; only 16 percent read word-by-word. So how do you train students to utilizing Internet information well? What are "information literacy skills"?

You probably rarely read webpages word by word yourself. That means you're already familiar with two very important strategies for reading on the Web—skimming and scanning. Skimming and scanning help you find the information you need, without reading everything on a Webpage. Skimming is glancing quickly over a text to get a general idea of the topic. When skimming:

- Quickly look over the entire page, focusing on any titles and headings.
- Look at the illustrations, diagrams, and captions. What do they describe?

Scanning is looking for key words and phrases that will give you the specific information you need. When scanning:

- Look for key words, headings, and terms in bold or italics that refer to information you need.
- Read the first and last sentences of the paragraphs on the page to see if they connect to information you need.

The amount of information available over the Internet, on the news, in newspapers, and in magazines and books is overwhelming for most adults, let alone children. Beyond just gaining webpage fluency, therefore, it is critical that students learn to find, analyze, use appropriately, and credit the information at their fingertips. These are information literacy skills, and the sooner we begin teaching them, the better students' chances are of succeeding in the Information Age.

Information literacy skills entail complex thinking and reasoning. These types of skills take time and practice to learn, and many students passing through your classes do not have strong information literacy skills, so be patient and encourage students to practice, practice, practice.

Many of the following information literacy skills and techniques can be taught by first discussing the concept, followed by modeling and guided practice. As students watch you and other students manage information, think aloud about what is being analyzed, and reach conclusions, they will begin to use similar strategies for themselves.

Keep in mind that many of these skills are defined as advanced thinking skills by Higher-Order Thinking Skills (HOTS) or Bloom's taxonomy criteria. The Bloom's taxonomy skill(s) used in each strategy are included in parentheses:

1. Identify if there is a need for information within a task (Comprehension):
   - Recognize when information is needed to solve a problem or develop an idea, concept, or theme.
   - Brainstorm multiple pathways for approaching a problem or issue.
   - Identify, organize, and sequence tasks and specific activities to complete an information-based project.

2. Locate, identify, categorize, and analyze information needed (Comprehension and Analysis):
   - Formulate questions based on information needs.
   - Use effective search techniques; use key words to search for information.
   - Analyze various sources for validity and overall relevance.
   - Read competently to understand what is presented.

3. Assess the information found (Analysis and Evaluation):
   - Evaluate the quality of information by establishing authority.
   - Determine age, accuracy, and authenticity.
   - Distinguish among opinion, reasoned arguments, and fact.

4. Organize the information (Application):
   - Learn how knowledge is organized.
   - Organize and store data in searchable formats.
   - Organize information for practical application.

5. Use information effectively to address the problem or task (Synthesis):
   - Create new information by synthesizing data from primary and secondary sources.
   - Integrate new information with existing knowledge.
   - Summarize information found in sources.

6. Communicate information and evaluate results (Application and Evaluation):
   - Present information in a product form.
   - Revise and update the product in ongoing evaluation.

7. Respect intellectual property rights.
   - Develop knowledge for how information and knowledge is produced.
   - Document sources using appropriate formats.

As you work through the information literacy skills with your students, remember that these are not the types of skills you can model and teach once and assume students will learn and utilize. You are building on skills they have already developed on their own. They require very advanced thinking and organizing skills, and therefore need multiple visits and hands-on/minds-on practice. Keep in mind that every classroom has a range of information literacy, and it is important for a teacher to assess prior knowledge before starting a unit on information literacy.

Once your students have basic skills on searching and navigating the Internet and strategies to manage and make sense of the information they find, you can begin using the Internet in your lessons, learning centers, and individual assignments and projects.

Precautions and Possible Pitfalls

 The Internet is a "time bandit" and without structure, and it is easy for kids to lose their direction and purpose. Here are a few hints:

1. Give them a few selected websites related to their unit (in worksheet form) that relate directly to the lesson. Never start lessons by having students only use search engines.

2. Require students to find very specific information, not just surf. A rubric might be appropriate here.

3. Always require students to write down the URLs of the sites they use for reports in a bibliographic format. You might teach them a cut-and-paste technique to help develop their bibliography or references.

4. Don't send the entire class to the same site at the same time. Once you get them started, encourage the development of search engine techniques.

5. When possible, try to preview sites or do the easy key word searches before students visit them.

Sources

Bloom, B. S. (1956). *Taxonomy of educational objectives, handbook I: The cognitive domain.* New York: David McKay Co Inc.

Burnett, C., & Wilkinson, J. (2005). Holy lemons! Learning from children's uses of the Internet in out-of-school contexts. *Literacy, 39*(3), 158–177.

Morkes, J., & Nielsen, J. (1998). Applying writing guidelines to web pages. Accessed April 26, 2006, at: http://www.useit.com/

 Strategy 67: For children with reading difficulties, text-to-speech software offers some of the benefits of shared reading.

What the Research Says

 Balajthy (2005) provides an overview of the text-to-speech (TTS) software technology and summarizes the research on the benefits of TTS for struggling readers. The different type of TTS software available are categorized and examined for sophistication, and information is given regarding how teachers can obtain electronic text material for use with TTS. Practical suggestions are provided for implementing and using TTS in the classroom setting.

Classroom Applications

 Reading aloud is often a primary component of early reading and literacy efforts. It is often the key factor in creating a motivating learning environment for young readers. TTS packages are designed to be able to read aloud from a variety of file types. The TTS software analyzes text using a system of phonics and other word-identification rules and reads it aloud through a voice synthesizer. Listeners are provided a synchronized visual and auditory presentation of the text as they see the text on the monitor and hear the spoken word at the same time. The reading speed can be adjusted based on the needs of the user.

The TTS concept sounds really interesting and numerous commercial TTS software packages are available. In addition, several can be downloaded free of charge on the Internet. The sophistication, quality, and price of packages vary widely.

Text is readily available in electronic form. A simple Internet search for "electronic text" will produce results. If you are looking for a specific text or subject, add its name to the search. Text from the Internet and from word processors can be used in addition to PDF files some TTS software can read. A variety of websites now make extensive collections of texts available in the public domain. Project Gutenberg is an example. The World Factbook of the U.S. CIA provides country profiles on every country in the world! Blackmask provides text of inauguration speeches by every U.S. president. The Internet Public Library provides Kidspace for elementary students and Teenspace for older students. Stories written and contributed by children are published at KidPub.

ReadPlease 2003 and HelpRead are available as free downloads, and they work well for basic and simple TTS purposes. The CAST eReader and TextHelp are moderately priced and provide more performance options. Kurzweil 3000 and WordSmith are more expensive and provide even more options. Some have optical character recognition (OCR) software that allows users to scan print text and convert it to digital files. PDF Aloud blends with Adobe Acrobat, enabling PDF documents to be read aloud.

A wide range of features available include different voices (male or female). Some allow users to select and copy text and paste it into a software window and hear it read aloud. Others include built-in Web browsers, dictionaries, lists of synonyms, or syllabic pronunciation to help with word identification. Here is a sampling of what is available.

1. Windows-Based Software

ReadPlease 2000 is a free text-to-speech package for Win95/98/NT.

- The ATRC has a tutorial on downloading and installing ReadPlease 2000 available (link: tutorial).

TextAloud MP3 converts any text into spoken words and MP3 files.

- Files may be listened to immediately, or saved to .wav or MP3 files to hear later at your convenience.
- TextAloud can be tried for 15 days free by downloading a fully functional demo at the Next Up Technology home page.

WriteAway 2000 from The Institute on Applied Technology of The Boston Children's Hospital and Information Services Inc.

- Word processor has built-in word prediction.
- Variable vocabularies and frequency settings are included.
- Various built-in text-to-speech options are offered.

Acapela Group has a variety of text-to-speech products:

- BrightSpeech TTS—part of Acapela's "High Quality text to speech" line.
- Elan Sayso TTS—part of Acapela's "High Quality text to speech" line.
- Babil TTS—part of Acapela's "High Density text to speech" line.
- Elan Tempo TTS—part of Acapela's "High Density text to speech" line.
- Text-To-Speech Systems by Lucent Technologies is also available in different languages—English (American), German, Chinese (Mandarin), Spanish, French, and Italian.

Clip&Talk for Windows 3.1x/95/98/NT, Windows-compatible sound card

- Adds speech capability to Windows applications. It is designed to work with any application that can put text on the clipboard.
- Download the trial version, which reads up to 600 words.

WinSpeech for Windows 3.1x/3.0N/95/98/NT; also available from PC WholeWare

- Will read text files and convert each word to a phonetic equivalent for more natural sounding speech.
- Supports DDE so that other Windows applications can send text to it for reading. Includes an expandable dictionary.

"Help Read" from The Hawaii Education Literacy Project

- Will automatically read clipboard text or .txt documents.
- Supports both English and Hawaiian language.
- The ATRC has a tutorial on downloading and installing HELP Read (link: **tutorial)**.

Bell Labs Text-to-Speech website

- Allows you to enter text online and explore text-to-speech.
- Links to some of the other text-to-speech and voice recognition products at Bell Labs.

"textHELP" by Lorien Systems

- TextHELP! has been specifically designed for people with reading and writing difficulties, especially dyslexia. It is a vocabulary support package that talks, types, checks spellings, corrects mistakes, and has word prediction.

AT&T Text-to-Speech website

- A demo of text-to-speech is available.
- Definition and vision of text-to-speech applications are offered.

TextSound 1.0 by ByteCool Software

- Converts text files to .wav format.
- Handles batch conversions.
- Recognizes voices from a number of other text-to-speech software packages.
- Free trial download is available from website.

2. Macintosh-Based Software

"Reading Mouse" from Dangerous Games

- "Reading Mouse" has an animated face that will read any text file to you in any Plaintalk voice.

"ULTimate Reader" for Windows 3.x/95 or Macintosh

- Reads digital text from any source with flexible voice and high-lighting combinations.

3. Standalone Text-to-Speech Tools

QuickLink-Pen and **QuickLink-Pen Elite** by WizCom Technologies USA

- This "reading pen" is a portable pen-shaped device that can scan a word and read it to the user.
- The Quick Link is available in English, French, Spanish, or Portuguese.

DecTalk Text-to-Speech speech synthesizers from Digital Equipment

- The Dectalk Express is an external/hardware synthesizer that can be used as an alternative to a PC sound card.
- The DecAccess 32 is an internal/software synthesizer that can be used with the sound card of your PC (usually a SoundBlaster sound card).
- Both have multilingual capabilities.

Precautions and Possible Pitfalls

 A wide range of books on tape and CD are commercially available that have a similar function to TTS technology. Because of this you might think TTS is becoming obsolete. Beyond access to these texts, however, TTS can provide audio access to other text sources beyond these commercial texts.

For Internet use, TTS seems to offer the greatest potential. Students log on, perform a search or access a website, and are supported by read-aloud software. In reality, a struggling reader might have problems making sense of a range of URLs that come up in a search. A fluent reader would have no problem but a struggling reader would need support to use the technology.

Struggling readers still might have trouble with content or vocabulary, so they would need support to work on Internet literacy. The TTS software itself might need to be taught, and the effort needed to teach TTS literacy might take more work than teaching the content you want students to learn.

Teachers need to carefully consider all these factors to decide whether the effort will truly provide a payoff in student learning. Be sure you experiment and explore the potential and pitfalls of the technology before buying into the TTS paradigm.

Source

Balajthy, E. (2005). Text-to-speech software for helping struggling readers. *Reading Online*. Available at: http://www.readingonline.org/

Strategy 68: Use the Internet to improve reading comprehension.

What the Research Says

Julie Coiro (2003) points out that today's youth have to deal with a whole slew of new illiteracies as new technologies emerge. She maintains that the traditional notion of reading must be greatly expanded as young students interact in technology, and reading teachers must be aware of the changing definition of literacy. The Internet is one result of this new technology, which can be confusing if students are only taught to comprehend traditional texts. Coiro (2003) observed that research shows students perceive Web-text reading differently from print reading, and many readers can thus become easily frustrated "when not instantly gratified in their rapid search for immediate answers" (p. 458). For example, young readers cannot seem to make the correct comprehension choices and are too hasty with random selections; reading teachers should be aware of how to teach these new illiteracies so that they can effectively prepare students for their own literacy futures.

Classroom Applications

Coiro (2003) draws on a model of reading comprehension outlined in the RAND Reading Study Group's report (2002). The report suggests that electronic texts have different characteristics from conventional texts that require different types of comprehension processes and a different type of instructional strategies. Corio (2003) characterizes the new texts as hypertextual networks, which, she maintains, have new types of story grammar and new formats. Teachers must now teach their students that the Web-based texts are *nonlinear, interactive,* and have *multiple media forms. Nonlinear* Web-based texts have hyperlinks embedded in short passages and readers are thus able to navigate their own reading pace and their own reading path, which is not an option in conventional, linear texts. The text is actually *interactive,* as the reader is able to interact and engage with the text in more personal ways.

In addition to these two features, Web-based texts are different from conventional texts presented in print and graphics media, which are two-dimensional. Web-based texts include many more types of media and symbols such as icons, animations, cartoons, and audio and video clips, not to mention lots of different font sizes. Coiro (2003) suggests that the reading teacher's role now becomes more of that of a facilitator who helps student access, manipulate, and respond to information on the Internet by getting them to take a critical stance toward these Web-based texts so that they can see biases embedded in the texts. She says that modeling these strategies is even more important when students are using the Internet. Reading teachers can, for example, model these strategies by asking (and answering) themselves in front of their students what explicit or hidden values are embedded in this Internet text, what types of media are being used, and how these shape the way the information is presented and interpreted.

Precautions and Possible Pitfalls

 In order for reading teachers to be able to model strategies to help their students manipulate and interpret Web-based text, they themselves must be proficient in use of the Internet; in fact, they may need to pursue their own professional development to become more proficient in Internet use, for example, to be able to demonstrate inferential reasoning skills to differentiate types of hyperlinks.

Sources

Coiro, J. (2003). Reading comprehension on the Internet: Expanding our understanding of reading comprehension to encompass new literacies. *Reading Teacher, 56*(5), 458–463.

RAND Reading Study Group. (2002). Reading for understanding: Towards an R&D program in reading comprehension. Retrieved June 9, 2006, from: http://www.rand.org/

 Strategy 69: Use electronic pen pals (ePALS) to have students communicate with people and sites beyond the classroom.

What the Research Says

According to Louanne Smolin and Kimberly Lawless (2003), a technologically literate person is someone who understands what technology is and how to use it with relative ease. As the

U.S. Department of Education suggests, they maintain that students must move beyond just knowing how to use technology such as computers and the Internet to being able to manipulate these technologies to increase academic performance. Reading teachers must thus be able to help their students become technologically literate by showing them how to use these technologies and how to express their ideas and communicate with diverse groups, similar to present language arts standards.

Classroom Applications

Smolin and Lawless (2003) suggest that by working in small-group activities, students' can learn to interact independently while at the same time learning from each other. Smolin and Lawless (2003) propose the use of ePALS.com (http:www.epals.com) on the Internet to foster such independence. ePALS is one of the largest online classroom communities in the world, and using such a communication tool allows teachers and students alike to locate electronic pen pals in all regions of the world and in many different languages. Teachers can have students perform basic communication skills such as developing e-mail communications, but they can also get students to work in groups or perform collaborative projects. Students can join weblogs and e-mentoring groups. This website translates from one language to another so students can communicate with others anywhere in the world, even though their "epals" many speak a different language. Teachers can set up common projects with other teachers and students from around the world, and they can all share and compare data on the same project from different contexts. According to Smolin and Lawless (2003), teachers can find collaborative projects across curriculum areas by using the Internet Projects Registry (http://gsh.lightspan.com/pr/index.html), which lists curriculum-based projects from a variety of organizations. Teachers can search for projects by subject area, age level, or project starting dates.

Precautions and Possible Pitfalls

Like all Internet-related projects, both students and teachers must be proficient not only in manipulating technology such as computers and the Internet, but also know how to critically interpret what is presented on the Web. Students must be monitored at all times while involved with Internet use. Most schools have some type of blocking software installed to restrict student access to certain Internet sites. You can set up some type of fair use technology policy to be shared with parents and students to alert them to the expectations teachers have for the students' Internet use.

Finally, unfortunately only those countries and schools that are linked to the Web can participate in creating such "epals" projects.

Sources

Smolin, L., & Lawless, K. (2003). Becoming literate in the technological age: New responsibilities and tools for teachers. *Reading Teacher, 56,* 22–29.

U.S. Department of Education. (1997). President Clinton's call to action for American education in the 21st century: *Technological Literacy.* Retrieved June 10, 2006, at: www.ed.gov/

Strategy 70: Use CD-ROM storybooks with early readers.

What the Research Says

Shirley Lefever-Davis and Cathy Pearman (2005) maintain that the world for young students is a different place today than it was for their teachers, as they are now surrounded with more opportunities to use technology from the very beginning of their education. They therefore suggest that reading teachers start their students reading early (K–2), and by the end of the second grade, students should be able to use developmentally appropriate multimedia resources to support learning. Lefever-Davis and Pearman (2005) suggest that electronic texts, such as CD-ROM storybooks, could be a great means for teachers to start beginning readers on technology that also advance the goals of their reading program. As they have observed, CD-ROM storybooks present young children's literature not only with traditional text and illustrations but also include other elements such as spelling analogies when they click on a word within a text to enhance the reading experience. By using CD-ROM storybooks, teachers can derive many benefits for their students' literacy development, as Lefever-Davis and Pearman (2005) have pointed out; electronic texts, for example, provide beginning readers with the ability to self-select and take more control over their own reading, and the animations provided in the CD-ROM storybooks further enhance comprehension by reinforcing the context through signaling story events and even the mood of the story itself.

Classroom Applications

Lefever-Davis and Pearman (2005) suggest reading teachers select CD-ROM storybooks with features that are specific to their instructional needs. For example, if the instructional goal is to increase reading comprehension, they should select CD-ROM texts that have features such as animations that occur automatically because they can help set the mood and establish a setting for the story, but if the instructional goal is only to decode information, then these same animations may distract the beginning readers from the text itself. Thus, reading teachers must remember that, when they use CD-ROM storybooks, they must keep focused on their instructional goals and also keep their young readers on task.

Precautions and Possible Pitfalls

Lefever-Davis and Pearman (2005) caution that reading teachers should be aware of the potential for CD-ROM storybooks to promote passive readers who let the computer do the work of reading because of an overreliance on electronic text features rather than actively engaging with the text. CD-ROM storybook features make decisions easy for the readers, as they can click on every available feature without making conscious decisions of their own. One more important pitfall is the cost not only of the CD-ROM storybooks themselves but also of all the computer equipment associated with their use. So reading teachers must decide if the added expense will be educationally worthwhile compared to cheaper traditional texts.

Source

Lefever-Davis, S., & Pearman, C. (2005). Early readers and electronic texts: CD-ROM storybook features that influence reading behaviors. *Reading Teacher*, *58*(5), 446–454.

Index

CORWIN PRESS

The Corwin Press logo—a raven striding across an open book—represents the union of courage and learning. Corwin Press is committed to improving education for all learners by publishing books and other professional development resources for those serving the field of PreK–12 education. By providing practical, hands-on materials, Corwin Press continues to carry out the promise of its motto: **"Helping Educators Do Their Work Better."**